Polly Toynbee is the *Guardian*'s social and political commentator. Previously she was the BBC's Social Affairs Editor and columnist for the *Independent* and the *Observer*. She is the author of *Hard Work: Life in Low-Pay Britain*, *Hospital* and *Lost Children*. With David Walker she has written two audits of Labour's first and second terms: *Did Things Get Better?* and *Better or Worse? Has Labour Delivered?*

David Walker is director of getstats, the campaign to boost numeracy. After a career in journalism he became communications director of the Audit Commission and is now contributing editor of *Guardian Public Leaders Network*. He is a member of the Economic and Social Research Council, and non-executive director of the Central & North-West London Foundation Trust. He co-authored *The Times Guide to the New British State* and *Sources Close to the Prime Minister*.

Dogma and Disarray

Cameron at Half-Time

Polly Toynbee and David Walker

First published in Great Britain in 2012 as an ebook by
Granta Books, Granta Publications, 12 Addison Avenue,
London W11 4QR

This is a limited print edition published by the authors.

3 5 7 9 8 6 4

CONTENTS

CHAPTER 1

Nothing short of a revolution

The 2012 Brighton arts festival enjoyed buoyant ticket sales. Visitors thronged to a bouquet of performances, installations and events. Outside the Dome on an early summer evening (when it wasn't raining) you might have surveyed the crowds and said we live in a happy enough land, laid back, coolly tolerant. Sponsors' wallets were shut tight, but audiences flocked to this annual flowering of dance, music and theatre on the south coast.

Questioned during 2011 about well-being by the Office for National Statistics (ONS) or about happiness by Ipsos MORI, three out of four people had been as positive, and looked likely to continue being so in 2012. The crowds were certainly out in force during the Jubilee weekend. And there was more to come. David Cameron's aversion to big government had not led him to staunch the £9.3 billion flow into 2012's great circus, the London Olympics.

But the economic facts tell a darker story. Disposable incomes were falling for a third year and households will not recapture their previous peak living standards till the end of the decade, said the Centre for Economics and Business Research. In May 2012 the economy fell into recession again with output unlikely to pass its 2008 level until 2014, a slump longer than the Great Depression.

For some, there was extra pressure. At Addenbrooke's Hospital in Cambridge contracted-out cleaners were sent a letter by their contractor employers, telling them to take a 21 per cent pay cut or face the sack: husband-and-wife night cleaners, facing a £600 a month cut between them, protested outside the hospital that they couldn't live on the new rates.

Other polls showed consumer confidence slipping as anxiety about jobs shot up the roster of public concerns. The same May, on the fourth floor of a block in Camden, we met an angry lorry driver. Voted Tory all his life, he said, but no longer. He had worked hard, paid his National Insurance, but now he had been struck down by a degenerative illness. Barely able to walk and instructed not to drive by his doctor, he had twice had his fitness tested by Atos, the French company awarded a government contract to assess work capacity. Yes, they said: having walked into the test centre he was evidently fit to work. The insulting suggestion that he was malingering was as hurtful as the loss of income. A couple of years ago he too might have applauded a cull of claimants. Now he had become one himself.

Scrounging – a sin committed only by those at the bottom of the income scale – is a strong Cameron theme. For all his suave charm, he has turned out to be a great hater. His is not a Britain at ease with itself. Recession has lowered the incomes of those in the middle against whom poverty is measured, so that although the technical measures were showing marginal improvement in overall inequality, no one is any better off. Life as lived in Cameron's country feels increasingly raw and unfair. He and his clique radiate privilege: they barely inhabit the same society as people at the bottom of the jobs and income distribution.

Median household income was stagnating well before the 2008 crash. Triumphant GDP growth in the century's first decade saw incomes soar for the top 10 per cent but their prosperity disguised how far that echelon was sucking up all the nation's growth. Yet for all Labour's collusion with the financiers responsible for wrecking the economy, its tax and benefits policies had channelled money towards low earners and tempered the forces pulling the distribution of income towards ever-greater inequality.

By 2010 the UK economy was picking up after its collapse and growing at 1.1 per cent. However Cameron and his chancellor George Osborne had a theory that gave state spending no credit for this recovery. In their view, welfare and public service jobs crowded out private enterprise. Now they had their moment, a heaven-sent opportunity to realize long-held fiscal, economic and political objectives. Crash, deficit and part-victory at the polls presented them with occasion and pretext to do faster and more brutally what in other financial circumstances they would have approached more cautiously: to dismantle the state.

Their cover story was that they had to apply the hot poultice of Thatcherism in order to win market confidence. Ratings agencies and bond traders would sustain UK national debt at low interest rates only if they could feel the pain. Tories and the opinion-formers of finance were in tune. Once, Harold Wilson had inveighed against shadowy union bosses who called the shots. Today's financiers are similarly closely knit and similarly politically motivated, but this prime minister welcomes their ideological bias. Markets are not wise or consistent, however, and confronted with the results of austerity in overdrive, fickle traders and ratings agencies were soon to change their tune.

Dogma and Disarray

In writing this half-time report on Cameron's occupation of Number Ten we found it difficult to weigh the strength of his determination to dismantle the state (dogma) against his confusion and incompetence in carrying it out (disarray). We tell ourselves political leaders know what they are doing when in fact they are often deeply confused. Cameron is often swept up by one day's headlines, in thrall to conflicting beliefs within his own party, navigating without maps and oblivious to the unintended consequences of his policies.

So his programme might be less grand design than instinct. But the urges were strong, giving the Tories identity and political impetus. Their tactics had been to cut back hard and get growth going in time for a general election in 2015. Spending cuts have sucked purchasing power out of the economy but the consequent 'rebalancing' hasn't happened. Sterling has lost a quarter of its value and though exports are suddenly more competitive, they have picked up only a little, nowhere near enough to fill the abyss of domestic demand. Aggregate growth collapsed again. Latest forecasts suggest borrowing in 2016–17 will be £24 billion, which is not much lower than the £26 billion forecast by Alistair Darling in his March 2010 budget. Despite Osborne's extra turns of the fiscal screw, the pain has yielded almost nothing. Where's Plan B? critics wailed. There is none, because the goal is not fiscal equilibrium but completion of what Margaret Thatcher began: nothing short of a revolution, the *Economist* said approvingly.[1] She had privatized the nationalized industries, but Cameron would privatize the state itself. She wasted her first term, Cameron believes, and is determined not to do the same. Hence his breakneck speed.

Once in Downing Street Cameron stripped off his green-tinged modernizer clothing. Incoming governments enjoy a media honeymoon and the Tory-dominated press ensured that for many months contradictions and broken promises went largely unremarked. The government U-turned all over the place. 'Failed and discredited', Osborne had called the Private Finance Initiative before the election, only for his Treasury to approve £17 billion worth of new PFI deals. No rise in Value Added Tax, Cameron had vowed; it rose. On Child Benefit he'd said, 'I wouldn't means-test it'; to qualify, families must now pass a strict test of means. They were going to keep the Educational Maintenance Allowance; it has disappeared. Of the thousands of extra midwives pledged, there's no sign. Days before polling Cameron had said, 'Any cabinet minister who comes to me and says "Here are my plans" and they involve frontline reductions, they'll be sent straight back to their department to go away and think again.'[2] None has been sent back, despite deep frontline cuts.

An obvious explanation for these somersaults is everyday political perfidy, but Cameron's opportunism is extreme; he seems remarkably unabashed at abandoning promises made to all and sundry. Beneath all the appurtenances of a relaxed, noblesse oblige Tory grandee of the old school, he has rigid beliefs. Ostensibly laid back, colloquial, personable, socially liberal, he doesn't have the cast of the fanatic in his eye. Yet his political generation pinned Thatcher posters on their walls, venerated Hayek and took their ideological ballast from the Republican right in the US. Where Thatcher was canny, at least till poll tax hubris brought her down, Cameron is indifferent to the nitty gritty of statecraft. His nonchalance borders on contempt: if the state is the problem, why worry about administering it badly? Osborne's March 2012 budget, which forced him into multiple U-turns, exemplifies the dilettantism that has become the Tory front bench style – he just could not be bothered to do his homework. The Commons' Public Administration Select

Committee, chaired by a Tory, said that to make change work you need a brain at the centre; you need information, resolution, leadership – and they have all been lacking.[3]

Education Secretary Michael Gove, intent on dismantling 150 years of English schools administration, has been one of the few effective at bending the machine to his radical will. In health, criminal justice and welfare the Cameron era has been characterized by the 2012 catchphrase 'omnishambles'. But perhaps all this serves a greater purpose. Confusion – or, in Cabinet Office minister Francis Maude's enthusiastic euphemism, 'administrative untidiness' – was welcome.[4] Market fanatics have long admired Joseph Schumpeter's idea of creative destruction: now it was to be adapted to the public sector.[5] How knowingly Tories went about destruction is debatable. Insiders say Cameron never got much beyond the cover sheet of the massive health restructuring proposed by Andrew Lansley. Paul Johnson, head of the Institute of Fiscal Studies (IFS), called their attitude to evidence cavalier: why, for example, didn't they pilot their health reforms in limited areas and measure the result?[6] The Tory reply is simple: you don't need to pilot an article of faith. Number Ten floats above detail; departments are not coordinated; ministers don't communicate. But if Cameron's guiding purpose is to downsize and diminish, to prove the state doesn't work, there may be more method in his ruling madness than meets the eye.

CHAPTER 2

The great deception

Friends and enemies agree that Cameron is not an ideas man; he is intuitive and presents himself brilliantly. It is Oliver Letwin, the shadowy Cabinet Office minister, who supplies the policy. Garrulous, he is rarely allowed out by the spin doctors. But his Mr Bean impersonations – he was caught dumping official papers in a bin in St James's Park – should fool no one: he was formerly special adviser to Thatcher's guru, Sir Keith Joseph. In his 'post-bureaucratic society' the state shrivels, pushed back to residual functions, which are then taken over by profit-making companies.

Letwin had confided to the party faithful in 2004 that the 'NHS will not exist under the Tories'.[7] It would merely be 'a funding stream handing out money to pay people where they want to go for their healthcare'. That captures the logic behind Lansley's health reform. During the 2001 election the press said Letwin had gaffed by blurting out that the Tories would cut enough to push the state down to 35 per cent of GDP. All he did was disclose page one of the war book.

But their bald intentions had to be wrapped in PR speak. The Tories had suffered three spectacular election failures. Tony Blair thought Britain an essentially conservative country that could only be cajoled or fooled into a little more generosity to the disadvantaged, but Cameron believed that twenty-first-century Britain was liberal and welfarist by instinct, most citizens proud of cradle-to-grave social supports and contemptuous of American social neglect, albeit with strong reservations about benefits for the working-age poor. For the Tories' 2005 manifesto Cameron had himself drafted the patient passport, which would let the well-off extract cash from the NHS to spend on private medicine, topped up with their own funds. It proved political poison. So Cameron, in presenting his party's plans for government, dressed the Thatcherite wolf in sheep's clothing, and very fetching it was on the political catwalk, at first.

His adviser Steve Hilton rebranded him, giving us Cameron with hoodies, Cameron with huskies and Cameron on a housing estate with the activist group Citizens UK (which subsequently failed to get the community organizing contract he promised them). Britain was broken, but this emollient figure would heal it. The cause of fracture was, of course, the state: it crowded out initiative, stifled endeavour, sapped the work ethic and smothered enterprise.

Enter the Big Society, Cameron's big idea for mass mobilization of voluntary and charitable effort. Bell Pottinger Public Affairs chairman Peter Bingle wondered admiringly at the 'deliberate strategy for it to be nebulous and inchoate'.[8] His success in phrasemaking had a lot to do with the gullibility of journalists, while think tanks and pundits competed fiercely to appear to be à la mode. All the Big Society did was to rebrand charitable and voluntary action, as if people would spontaneously give up profiteering and rigging markets and turn altruistically to do good by their fellow citizens – in which case Big Government could safely be shrunk. Then came the astonishing admission by the Big Society tsar, Lord Wei, that he 'could not afford' to continue his own voluntary service because he needed to make money.[9]

'Giving' lasted as a theme until Osborne's fateful March 2012 budget, when his cut in tax relief for big donors exposed how rich people would only contribute to the Big Society if they were bribed with tax reductions. Tory Party treasurer Peter Cruddas had to resign when he boasted Big Giving meant Big Access, as if adding to party coffers was itself the way to build the Big Society.[10]

'Nudge' was another flaky concept – the highly unoriginal idea that governments could get people to change their ways indirectly, by persuasion and incentives. Gemma Harper, Chief Social Scientist at the Department for the Environment, Food and Rural Affairs (Defra), told a House of Lords inquiry that 'behaviour change is very much used as a shorthand for alternatives to regulation and fiscal measures'.[11] Fiscal measures mean taxes and the government wanted less of them.

Like its predecessor, the government was infatuated with *choice* but, unlike Labour, was not going to be too unhappy if lack of choice led to impatience and frustration with public services, for that would prove that the state was unreliable and incompetent. Free schools saw the most extravagant rhetoric. Gove's line was that even the poorest had the choice to spend their time and treasure setting up schools in opposition to state primaries, knowing very well, as indeed it turned out, that this was a choice only the better off had the means to seize: three-quarters of free schools took fewer deprived pupils than the local average.[12]

Free schools were *localist* – another Cameron cry taken

9

over from Labour and given an ideological twist. 'Of course,' Cameron conceded, 'some argue that the greatest power of all would be to let local government raise more of its own revenue and decide how to spend it.' Except the one thing Osborne and the Treasury do not want is fiscal imagination and local government tax-raising activism. Instead they arm-twisted councils to freeze council tax for two years.

Tory localism took a curious form since there was no let-up in directives from ministers: a push from Cameron for elected city mayors, orders from Communities Secretary Eric Pickles about exactly when councils should empty bins, barked instructions on what council executives should be paid and on things ministers cared about such as adopting a tough Whitehall-devised scorecard on local performance. Little wonder confusion reigned and the turnout in the May 2012 referendums on mayors was derisory. No sooner did policing minister Nick Herbert promise to 'end centralization, targets and ring fences' than he decreed police forces must follow orders on buying and running helicopters and IT. Just to be on the safe side, he issued instructions on the purchase of constables' shirts and shields too. The police and crime commissioners voters are being invited to vote for in November (in England outside London and in Wales) have been squeezed into insignificance between an interventionist Home Office and the private contractors lined up to take over large slices of policing: citizens are unlikely to flock to the polls in elections that look like an inconsequential gimmick.

Localism did not mean interfering with Tesco-sized big business. Tory thinking says: break down the state, but not other sources of centralized national power, big banks, merged companies, media empires or wealth. Cameron and colleagues were alert to the dangers of carrying their own logic to extremes. The chief executive of a solid Tory county council explained to us how in the first flush of Big Society enthusiasm, officers had worked up a plan to close libraries and abandon the youth service, exhorting the 'community' to pick them up or let them die. They went further, suggesting villagers take control of speed detection, arming themselves with hand-held radar and publishing the registration numbers of speeding vehicles on the Internet. Tory headquarters took fright and soon put a stop to that.

CHAPTER 3

Fellow travellers

We are calling it the Cameron government because his coalition partners agreed with everything of real importance to the Tory programme. They agreed with the two great planks of the platform: to carry out deficit reduction at a reckless pace and the bigger project of deconstructing the state. The Liberal Democrats echoed Osborne's extravagant scaremongering about Greek-style risk. Across swathes of policy, even Hercule Poirot could not detect much Liberal Democrat influence, especially on Tory signature issues such as crime and immigration. The most glaring example of complicity is the NHS. Before the election some leading Liberal Democrats had out-Toried the Tories in their frustration with a state-run, tax-funded service, calling for co-funding with private contributions.[13] Policies the Liberal Democrats labelled as their own were often the most jumbled. Nick Clegg claimed credit for a pupil premium, adding to per capita spending on pupils from disadvantaged backgrounds; while it will help some poorer schools, by and large it is likely to benefit Tory and Liberal Democrat areas by moving cash out of cities into the shires.

Conceding crumbs to his junior partner, the Tory leader secured for himself and his party the principal offices of state, control of public finances and the direction of economic policy.[14] Not a bad deal. Andrew Adonis noted Clegg's claims to have prevented the repeal of the Human Rights Act but 'he has not stopped any notable aspect of Osborne's pre-election economic plan'.[15]

Clegg lost his shirt over constitutional change. First, the promised referendum was on the alternative vote for MPs, rather than the proportional representation he favoured. Secondly, reform of voting for the House of Commons did not just fail to get Cameron's support; the Tories mobilized, giving £660,000 and lending their headquarters to the No campaign to ensure the cause was ignominiously defeated. Clegg agreed to a partisan set of changes to House of Commons constituency boundaries in exchange for a half promise to democratize the House of Lords, which now looks as likely to be realized as Clegg's winning the next election.

Disgruntled Tory backbenchers, losing opportunities for ministerial advancement to their disliked coalition partners, grumbled that Cameron actually preferred coalition, as it allowed him to be socially liberal and ignore their gut conservatism, on matters such as a bonus for married couples. No doubt Cameron would prefer to have won outright, but negotiations to set up the coalition showed him how he might gain in the new political circumstances. The more Clegg talks about social mobility, fairness and green policies the better, as he cloaks the true direction of the Cameron project. Clegg speeches may create problems with dimmer Tory backbenchers, but serious players understand the Liberal Democrats for what they are: useful idiots.

CHAPTER 4

The convenient calamity

With Saatchi-sharp PR skill, Cameron and Osborne localized the global crisis and made it 'Labour's mess'.[16] They traded on the electorate's rejection of Gordon Brown, the indisputable fact of the collapse of Britain's big banks and the hole in the public finances caused by economic recession in 2008–9. With nursery-level economics, the Tories and their political allies lodged debt reduction in the collective imagination as an urgent necessity, trading on pre-Keynesian notions to support a 1930s fiscal policy that had driven slump into a deeper depression.

The attack on Labour was doubly dishonest. In opposition Tories (and Liberal Democrats) had promised to match Labour's increased spending on public services, especially health and education. In *The Verdict*[17] we showed why Brown had not bridged the gap between revenues and spending. The IFS compared the UK unfavourably – if with the benefit of hindsight – with countries that did use the years of plenty to bolster their balance sheets. So, it would have been just to charge Labour with *under-taxing*.

Fiscal duty could be done by raising tax; there's evidence that tax increases depress economic activity less than spending cuts. In the event Osborne had no choice but to raise tax somewhat in his 2010 budget. But antipathy to taxation was what led Osborne to rush into cutting the top rate of income tax in his March 2012 budget, at a substantial cost to his party's popularity.

The UK economy was a mess because it was lopsided and over-dependent on banks. For that a good portion of the blame can be visited on Thatcher, whose 'Big Bang' deregulation of the City in 1986 stripped constraints away from the banks. But instead of a flourish of enterprise and growth, they traded in ever-riskier financial assets. Boardrooms built themselves a structure of mutual rewards that even Cameron and Osborne had reluctantly to admit was dysfunctional as well as morally repugnant. Big Bang had fiscal consequences, too, as it led the Treasury to rely increasingly on a bloated financial sector. When the banks boomed, its coffers were replenished, but if the financial sector were ever to fail we risked a more drastic loss of state income than in other countries with less monolithic economics. Instead of recalibrating and diversifying the economy, Blair and Brown rode the cresting wave of finance. The latter, in his folly, said the boom would last for ever, but the tide began to ebb outside branches of Northern Rock in September 2007.

Before the election Osborne gave the impression he welcomed the crisis. Claiming the UK's fiscal position was like Greece's sent out a dangerous message to world markets, and the analogy was spurious: UK debt was long-term, denominated in the national currency and mostly owed to UK citizens. A cleverer comparison would have been with Japan, where national debt had exceeded

GDP for decades without malign consequences. The gilts market was buoyant because the UK ranked high on the league tables for security. What's more, the IFS noted wisely, 'economic theory provides little practical guidance on the optimum level of public debt'.[18] But the Tories wanted a dramatic pretext for cutting spending and benighted Greece fitted the bill perfectly. For them it was a perfect storm. Cameron had backers. The Bank of England governor, Mervyn King, is standing proof of the Tory proclivities of the economic establishment. Cut spending and sharply, was his welcome message: make space for a private-sector-led recovery. Like all too many other professional economists, the governor was stuck inside the iron cage of a discipline that had not foreseen the collapse and could not explain it. But not so the *Financial Times*. The paper's former economics commentator Samuel Brittan had spelled it out. 'If we have a normal economic recovery the red ink will diminish remarkably quickly,' he wrote. 'If we don't, it won't and won't need to.'[19] The observation was prescient. His successor Martin Wolf repeated the prescription. Himself no great friend of public spending, he argued consistently and with vim that cutting demand in a weak economy, subject to the vicissitudes of the Eurozone crisis, was unmitigated folly.

The creation of the Office of Budgetary Responsibility (OBR) in 2010 proved they weren't dogmatic, the Tories said: they were willing to submit to the forecasts of an independent body. Except its remit was limited, and it too went with the consensus in its early months. Brittan, Wolf and the American Nobel laureates Paul Krugman and Joseph Stiglitz railed against consensus economics because it was voodoo economics. Cutting spending, they said, does not lead to more growth. On the contrary, the historical record said the opposite. But that's religion for you: it was a matter of faith that cutting and growth are profoundly and indissolubly related. The empirical evidence since 2010 confirms that, if anything, cutting has an inverse relationship with growth in conditions of economic depression: that's the message from Greece, the Republic of Ireland or Spain, just as it was for Keynes in the UK eighty years ago. But claiming cuts cause recovery served a prime purpose: to get rid of as much public spending as these opportune circumstances would allow.

In 2010, everyone, leftish and right, orthodox and dissenter, agreed that the public finances had to be put in order. The critical questions were over how long a period; with what regard to changing economic circumstances at home and abroad; and which bits of the national waistline were to be pinched. Osborne's fiscal tightening demanded £113 billion be shed and he went hell for leather for a plan weighted, four to one, in favour of spending cuts over tax increases. That predestined those who most used public services or most needed benefits to suffer the most, while a decision to balance the books via higher taxes would have fallen on the broader shoulders. That meant Osborne knew his repeated claim 'We're all in it together' was nonsense. That phrase became his albatross, shot down during his 2012 budget when higher-rate taxpayers had their 'burden' relieved: millionaires were given a £14,000 tax break. Within the spending cuts, the Tories chose to take the lion's share out of welfare benefits going to poorer families. As for the cuts in public spending, the IFS's Johnson called them a 'hotchpotch'. What calculus lay behind cutting education by 11 per cent, maintaining health spending in real terms and still building aircraft carriers for which the Ministry of Defence could not afford planes?

Governments, like boats, grow barnacles. Every so often the ship needs a good scrape. Whoever took power in 2010 ought to have chiselled away at consultants, temps, property costs, padded IT bills, and top pay and pensions. The IFS and other commentators go further and say that after a sustained period of increases in public spending under Labour, the scope for cuts had grown; so, they calculate, the spending cuts planned by the Cameron government would take totals back to their 2004–5 real terms total. But crude aggregates ignore the distribution of winners and losers. Need does not stand still over eight years; for example, numbers of old people are growing. Public spending affects fairness; cutting it back will have consequences for equality, both actual and perceived, especially if everyone else sees their own real living standards falling back while the top 1 per cent have a tax cut.

Because, deep down, taxes are anathema to Tories, what they said and did in half their fiscal policy lacked drive and was pocked with anomalies. The proclaimed need to balance the books could have been an occasion for cleaning up a vast and clumsy tax regime. Page after page had been added as lobbyists claimed exemptions. HM Revenue & Customs (HMRC) added to the rules every time it had to close ever more aggressive tax avoidance dodges devised by the same big accountancy firms battening on the government for consulting contracts. But instead of tax reform and simplification, Osborne and a conservative Treasury have done as little as possible. They did take a levy on banks in 2010, but it was only a one-off and Osborne simultaneously reduced corporation tax, promising business more cuts to come. Ripe fiscal fruit hung there to be picked, but Osborne hid his secateurs. The government fought against the financial transaction tax prized in Berlin and Paris as a way of controlling market madness and a source of revenue. Osborne could have cut exemptions from inheritance tax, but he had made his name in 2007 with a pledge to cut taxes on inheritance, which are paid on only 6 per cent of the wealthiest estates. Above all, he could have got to grips with the fair taxation of property. Labour had funked property tax through the years of booming house prices while the Liberal Democrats feebly called for a levy on ultra-expensive homes, dubbed the mansion tax. Osborne increased tax on house sales through stamp duty in the 2012 budget for higher-cost properties but ducked the substantive issue of taxing property itself; his welcome effort to catch tax avoiders buying property through special companies was only a sideshow.

His 2010 budget raised VAT to 20 per cent. It might have been less damaging to consumption to keep the lower rate but expand the list of goods and services to which VAT applies: a lower proportion of consumer spending is subject to VAT in the UK than elsewhere. He might have tackled VAT exemptions enjoyed by financial services or increased VAT on domestic fuel, cushioning the squeeze for poor households with incentives for households to insulate, boosting the domestic economy with a scheme like Warm Front – but he abolished that. Such action would have required a coherent and radical approach to 'green taxation'. Instead this overconfident chancellor reckoned[20] that someone who had got the public to swallow big spending cuts could slip through modest tax increases on hot pasties or middle-income grannies: he was wrong.

The centrepiece of the 2012 budget was the cut in the top rate of income tax. This was a political judgement. The Treasury said: we're not raising much, because people have avoided paying the higher rate; they will stop avoiding it if they only have to pay a lower rate. Such calculations, the IFS caustically observed, assumed no continuing avoidance on the part of those who acquired a taste for avoiding the 50p rate. But Osborne had to raise taxes, so by not adjusting thresholds people were pushed into higher brackets: between 2011 and 2014, the number paying tax at 40p will rise from 3.7 million to 5 million. The government was deeply ambiguous and in other ways showed scant enthusiasm for getting the tax revenues in. Parliamentary theatre become comedy in November 2011 when the Public Accounts Committee, exasperated by officials' refusal to be frank about their negotiations with a major tax avoider, Goldman Sachs, insisted the HMRC lawyer in front of them swear an oath to tell the truth. A hapless clerk had to be sent wandering the corridors for a bible.

Instead of exempting HMRC from spending cuts, the government insisted on chopping its budget by a quarter and sacking 10,000 staff despite evidence that their investigations were netting up to £15 for every £1 spent on staff. The target is an extra £7 billion a year by 2015, which is barely a fifth of what HMRC itself estimates as the gap between what taxpayers owe and what it collects. The National Audit Office (NAO), using Whitehall's favourite phrase, said HMRC faced 'a significant challenge' in cutting staff costs while increasing revenues. Even if the notoriously hard-to-calculate tax gap were nearer the official £35 billion than the £125 billion figure estimated by Richard Murphy, director of Tax Research, thousands more staff could gainfully be employed. Meanwhile Letwin boasted that Whitehall employee numbers were now the lowest they had been since the Second World War.

Osborne signed a tax treaty with the Swiss in 2011 that will allow avoiders years to switch their money from alpine chalets to tropical tax havens, or the sodden Isle of Man. The enormity of this anomalous island in the Irish Sea is growing ever larger, with the UK continuing to sustain a worldwide string of tax havens. HMRC got the message that in dealing with giant corporates they should soft pedal: inspectors doubtless read the interview with the Cabinet Office minister, saying it was a 'compliment' for the UK to be described as a tax haven.[21] As the Euro wobbled in the spring of 2012, London drew yet more of the world's hyper-wealthy, and Greek shipowners and Italian plutocrats bought Mayfair and Knightsbridge property as a safe haven for cash: prices soared. The prime minister even made a tasteless joke in the hearing of the new president about welcoming escapees from higher wealth taxes in France. Responding to the revelation that scores of stars, footballers and others were salting away millions each in what was known as the K2 avoidance scheme, Cameron, as ever shooting from the hip, reprimanded Jimmy Carr, the first name to surface. But here was typical disarray: when he was instantly asked to condemn Gary Barlow, Tory-supporting Take That star, for indulging in the same wheeze, Cameron clammed up. He hadn't paused to consider how many large Tory donors, or indeed some of his own front bench, had used avoidance schemes. Britain remains the only Western country where the non-domiciled need not pay tax on foreign assets and income, for the slender price of £50,000 a year.

CHAPTER 5

Banking on growth

In delayed reaction to the financial crash and the obduracy of bankers rewarding themselves with outrageous bonuses, the public were worried about fairness. Labour had lost the election, but the Tories had at least to pretend to assuage widespread resentment over unjust rewards. But the same ambiguity that marked their approach to tax showed up in their treatment of finance and – the very respectability of the phrase signalled the change in mood – the unappealing faces of British capitalism. The Cameron government was fated to be disappointed by its business friends when the economy did not grow despite the spending cuts, but also to disappoint them by crowd-pleasing criticism of top pay.

During 2011, protest welled up. Tent dwellers took over the steps of St Paul's Cathedral, winning surprising approval. UK Uncut occupied Top Shop, Barclays, Boots and Vodafone, companies notorious for paying scant tax, and even right-wing newspapers were prepared to run headlines critical of corporate tax-avoiders. As FTSE 100 boardrooms signed themselves cheques for an average 49 per cent increase in pay in austerity year 2011, Cameron and Osborne had at least to express disapproval. The 2012 Queen's Speech promised to make shareholder votes on boardroom remuneration binding but stonewalled on the proposal to make directors' pay subject to a threshold vote requiring 75 per cent shareholder support and rejected entirely the suggestions of leavening remuneration committees with employee representatives, let alone benchmarking directors' pay to a ratio of average staff pay.

Reform of banking has been lethargic. Cameron and Osborne showed no inclination to examine the root causes of the banking crisis, City cultures or systems: not for them measures to break up existing interests and enforce competition. An insiders' inquiry led by Sir John Vickers gave them cover in refusing to separate retail from investment banking – beyond some paper-thin Chinese walls inside the big finance houses. Cameron and Osborne never contemplated a proportionate, albeit radical, remedy, which would have been to break up the big banks' oligopoly.

So the banks went on not lending to small business. Ecospin, a Midlands firm making electric vehicles, could not fulfil an order from Singapore because it could not get a line of credit, despite exhortations from the government to pick up export opportunities. Managing director Paul Loomes wasn't complaining about red tape or government bureaucracy: the banks were the block on enterprise. 'Their business is all about taking risk but they won't take any,' he complained.[22] Not for Cameron and Osborne the imaginative response of creating, say, an industrial bank, organized on regional lines, learning from and improving on German models.

After mentally spending years in the neo-liberal wilderness, indifferent to the fate of firms and sectors because 'market forces ruled OK', Labour had in its final months begun talking about 'rebalancing' the economy. Cameron was torn between the commitment to roll back the state and the pleading voices of business (including bankers) whose own free market views never precluded opportune bailouts or business-friendly government schemes. The government deployed a surviving Tory practitioner of intervention, Michael Heseltine, as a sort of ghostly adviser. But there was no map, no consistency: they refuted any connection made between the fate of firms and broader financial policy.

By instinct the government was hands-off, promising to slash the red tape allegedly holding business back. But in the real world, market failures had to be taped up. Take retailing, where the Tories' traditional closeness to Tesco, Sainsbury and Asda (based on lobbying, exchange of personnel and corporate donations) had to acknowledge the public's growing suspicion of the grocers' cartel. In response to the Competition Commission's finding that the supermarkets' dominance was bad for suppliers, ministers proposed a code of conduct. This might have prompted a root-and-branch look at retailing and the urban scene. The government agreed that high streets needed rejuvenating. PR savvy, they appointed Mary Portas as shopping tsar. But what followed was underfunded and disjointed. A new licensing Act let councils restrict alcohol sales, but what might have been a good move had no context. Sometimes, it's true, coherence just has to give way to political necessity. Free trading and anti-interventionist, the government still stopped the export of the drug sodium pentobarbital to the US to be used in executions, in the face of public revulsion.

A report from a Cameron business ally, Adrian Beecroft, was much more to Tory taste. He demanded freedom for employers to sack staff at will. Ministers wanted to increase the qualifying period for unfair dismissal, making claims more difficult: the plan under consultation will make anyone appealing to an employment tribunal pay as much as £600, and the maximum they can win is to be cut from unlimited compensation to around £30,000. A partisan approach, however, sat uncomfortably with rhetoric about sharing the national sacrifice. As Tory columnist Camilla Cavendish put it, 'asking a super rich Tory donor to write a report on how to dismantle workers' rights was not the best way to rally people behind the idea Britain's employment laws need to change'.[23] Employment tribunals did need to streamline and cut costs. But General Motors decided to continue building cars at Ellesmere Port not because the Cameron government was tearing up employment protection but because, with a gun to its head, a unionized Merseyside workforce had no choice but to agree less favourable terms and conditions.

The government's 'business can do no wrong' philosophy did not mesh with their worry that too few people are getting decent vocational training, especially through apprenticeships. Employers themselves warned of the paradox of joblessness and skills shortage, fearing the recession was being 'wasted' in terms of anticipatory vocational training. Business still had to be bribed to train employees, however, though a degree of confusion was revealed when, as part of a review by the Department of Business, Innovation and Skills (BIS) of impediments to growth, it was persuaded to exclude firms with fewer than 250 people from the employees' right to request time off to train and acquire skills. With one hand the government cut the further education budget by a quarter. With the other it expanded adult apprenticeships by 75,000 more than the level bequeathed by Labour and introduced a (small) scheme offering loans to adults aged over 24 training for qualifications. Yet many of the new apprenticeships amounted to only minor retraining for adults already in work, rebranding Labour's axed Train to Gain scheme.

Philosophical consistency was hard to sustain. If, as Business Secretary Vince Cable claimed, 'the UK already has one of the world's most flexible, adaptable labour markets [and] stands up very well in international comparisons', why wasn't business booming, especially now that the state was in retreat? The government had no cover story for when markets did not work to British advantage and it felt obliged to launch, for example, an Advanced Manufacturing Supply Chain Initiative to 'ensure more components can be sourced in this country'. When confronted with a multinational threatening to shift capital abroad, the Cameron government resorted to state bribes, like other countries. Some 1,400 jobs were threatened when the transport minister decided to buy German trains instead of ordering from Bombardier, a Canadian firm based in Derby. Such a loss of capacity in engineering caused shockwaves that pushed even free marketeers beyond their comfort zone. Another contract to build carriages was hastily assembled (Nissan was also a beneficiary from this reflex response). If there were no indigenous IT industry, if corporate decisions about UK employment were mostly taken overseas, did ministers care? When one of the few remaining British IT companies, Logica, was sold to Canada[24] the silence was deafening.

John Longworth, Director General of the British Chambers of Commerce, complained 'there is a big black hole when it comes to aiding business to create enterprise, generate wealth and grow'.[25] But wasn't a plan for growth an oxymoron? Government had cleared space but companies were not moving in, both for lack of credit and because consumer demand was too weak to risk investment and recruitment of staff.

Ministers had to admit a need for coordination and state intervention, if coyly. David Willetts, minister for universities and science, talked of bringing such sectors as aerospace, vehicle engineering, e-infrastructure and synthetic biology together inside 'leadership councils'. But Cameron never explained, not least to the firms that were to be shepherded into such anti-competitive behaviour, how government was simultaneously to be removed yet expected to instigate and lead investment and science-based development.

Opportunities for collaboration abounded, notably in equipping the country with fast fibre-optic broadband connections. Peter Cochrane, ex-head of R&D at BT, compared government proposals for communications to lighting a candle 'while the rest of the world is using a light bulb'.[26] The government tinkered. After Project Merlin failed to get the banks to lend to small business, they were urged to set up a joint Business Growth Fund promising £2.5 billion for small and medium enterprises: it took a year to start lending, and will be making just 25 loans in 2012. A pint pot of just £150 million, known as the Enterprise Finance Guarantee scheme, would 'leverage significant equity investment' into small business. A further £200 million targeted high-growth companies and the commercialization of new technologies – but wasn't this what those highly rewarded investment bankers should be doing? Another petty parcel was dedicated to small business finance.

Opportunities ought to arise from energy and the environment. The German government, for example, having decided against nuclear generation, was poised to invest huge sums in a new transmission system to carry energy from further investment in wind power. Controversial and difficult, but it had a vision. In the UK both companies and power-hungry households sought in vain for resolution and leadership. The Danish wind turbine maker Vestas pulled out of proposed investment in a factory in Sheerness in June 2012 blaming uncertainty about future orders.

'Vote Blue Go Green', Cameron had said. But it's hard to find a thread in Tory policy, even a consistent pro-business line in, for example, trying to defer existing commitments on renewable electricity by lobbying against a proposed EU Directive. The Tories did put £3 billion into a Green Investment bank, supposed to back renewable technology, though it was not a real bank, as any borrowing would add to state borrowing figures. Labour's Warm Front initiative had subsidized domestic energy efficiency measures, which the government sought immediately to recreate as the Green Deal, except with less money and less benefit for poorer households. (Only a third of private-rented properties with cavity walls had them insulated, against four out of ten owner-occupied dwellings and half of social units.)

The UK faces an energy gap that will have to be filled by some mix of renewables and nuclear. Cameron prevaricated. Ministers were reluctant to push onshore wind power in the face of his nimby rural backbenchers; while cutting incentives for solar installations they also dithered over the commitment to build new nuclear reactors bequeathed by Labour. No wonder one putative nuclear contractor, the German company RWE, pulled out and another, the French state-owned firm EDF, showed every sign of packing up and leaving Hinkley Point to the birds.

Tory nimbyism seemed to explain the speedy killing of the Labour-era regional development agencies (RDAs): their purpose was to attract investment and stimulate the economy in the North, where Labour was stronger. (The only RDA left intact was in London, under the control of the Tory mayor Boris Johnson.) But austerity and recession showed that prosperity was as badly distributed around England as ever. For the RDAs, which the record showed had pushed jobs and growth in places markets were reluctant to reach, albeit at high cost, the government substituted local enterprise partnerships. But these are non-statutory, without money or staff and not designed to address uneven development. A fraction of the RDA budget, £1.4 billion, was allocated to a new Regional Growth Fund that gave grants to entrepreneurs with bright ideas, provided they could convince those businesspeople the government had asked to distribute the money, which was restricted to areas deemed overly dependent on the public sector. At a likely cost per job of £33,000, the NAO recommended robust monitoring.[27]

England's regional question is really about the gap between London and the South East, and the rest. Governments can encourage firms to expand and people to move there, or try to push them out, to benefit less buoyant parts. Similarly, the big question in transport is whether to convey more people in and into London, or help them get more quickly to the Midlands and North. At first the government seemed to have made up its mind, planning a very expensive railway line going to Birmingham and then to Yorkshire, though the first train was unlikely to arrive on Platform 1 at Leeds station till 2025 at the earliest. Ready to go in 2010, High Speed Two was delayed again and again, with rows from nimby Tory MPs over its route through their constituencies, with the government studiously avoiding the decision on whether HS2 would ever link to HS1, the route from London to the Channel, for fear of upsetting yet more Tory MPs. These railways were the mainstay of a new National Infrastructure Plan, but this was no more than a hurried pulling together of projects already in the pipeline, several aimed at expanding capacity in the South East, such as Crossrail and the Thameslink improvement project. The government even created a 'National Skills Academy for Rail Engineering' backed by £2.7 million of public money, plus £2.2 million from companies, to train the workforce to build them. But Tim O'Toole, chief executive of First Group, complained that 'stealth cuts' to spending on public transport were limiting prospects and constraining growth. Councils, faced with grant cuts, were lopping subsidies to bus operators, such as First Group, which posted profit warnings. 'If you want people to travel to jobs, go to job interviews and all the rest of it, you have to have a vibrant bus network that people have access to.'[28]

But leading Tories tend not to take buses, Margaret Thatcher once remarking that to do so after the age of 25 was a sign of failure. They did fly, but on taking office, mindful of suburban votes, they tore up Labour's pledge to build a third runway at Heathrow airport. So was there a plan for redistributing air traffic or to staunch growth in aircraft movements? No. They dropped a proposal to levy flight duty on aircraft rather than individual passengers. Noises off from Boris Johnson about a mega-airport scheme in the Thames estuary exposed Tory indecision: his grand project was touted as self-financing, but was bound to cost huge amounts of public money. A new airport to the east of London was not necessarily a crazy idea, having long been advocated by the eminent urbanist Sir Peter Hall, but where did it fit into an England-wide scheme for transport and growth, let alone one for the whole UK?

The answer was that a 'scheme' made no sense when the state was being dismembered and sold off or contracted out piecemeal to companies. Privatization remained a gut instinct for the Tories, seemingly as strong now as when the Major government pushed through its disastrous privatization of the railways, which became a device for pumping public money straight into private train firms' balance sheets. Further thwarting the ostensible aim of privatization – to bring in competition to drive down costs – the Department of Transport was now proposing longer franchises for railway companies and amalgamating trains and track operations in regional monopolies.

BANKING ON GROWTH

At first Cameron forced the pace on privatization, then blamed his hapless Environment Secretary Caroline Spelman for misjudging the public mood over the proposed sale of 258,000 hectares of Forestry Commission land. After an instant and vociferous reaction from walkers, woodland groups and the National Trust, Spelman was wheeled out to say 'we got this one wrong'. The government regrouped, going after the helicopter search and rescue service provided by the RAF and air traffic control, where the Treasury is eyeing a £250 million gain from selling the state's remaining 49 per cent. Slices of another valuable public asset, electromagnetic spectrum, are being proffered to telecoms firms at pals' prices. The government abolished the Central Office of Information in its cull of quangos, and within months was touting government PR and publicity contracts to advertising agencies and public affairs companies. With postal services, which Labour had started preparing for sale, a private buyer would get equipment, routes and a workforce, but would not be required to cover their pensions, which would remain a state liability. A buzzword for Tory ministers was 'mutualism'. They extolled the John Lewis model, conveniently forgetting that the firm's founder John Spedan Lewis had donated his retail empire to his staff. Cameron was not so magnanimous: given a chance with the Post Office and Royal Mail, he proposed to reserve a puny 10 per cent of equity, which they would have to buy into. The Audit Commission was another example of talk and no action. Ministers promised auditors could form a mutual and take over the quango's work checking council accounts; in the event it was all contracted out to profit-seeking firms. The Canal and River Trust, which took over British Waterways in England, was neither a private company nor a mutual. Instead, pension liabilities were again retained on the state's books, and the canals and £460 million of assets passed to a giant unaccountable non-profit body. Property speculators are already buzzing round the honeypot.

But since 2010, sharper investors have been looking for pickings elsewhere. Cameron and Osborne have a fiscal policy – to cut spending – but no economic policy, in the sense of a strategy for promoting investment, upping productivity or renewing the basic services such as trains and airports that business says are a precondition for growth. What they do have is a sure-fire way for firms to make money. Cameron is opening up a vast new field for private profit, not by selling assets but by bringing firms into territory formerly considered fundamental to the state's identity, in crime and justice, schooling, universities and even the NHS.

CHAPTER 6

The ultimate privatization

Astonishment greeted the publication of the NHS plan in July 2010. Cameron had repeatedly promised not just to cherish the health service but the Coalition Agreement specifically vetoed 'top down re-organization'. But now came this upheaval, just when the NHS would be under greater financial pressure than ever before. Reading the plans, the NHS chief executive Sir David Nicholson later confessed he felt 'denial, anger and depression'.[29] What he failed to understand or, as a loyal civil servant, could not publicly acknowledge, was that Lansley was not whimsical or unstrategic but was making the NHS the pioneer for privatization across the public services. Lansley had told him it was revolutionary.[30] If it could be accomplished in the NHS, the most politically sensitive of all public services, then the field was open.

Two years on, the risks Cameron is running with the NHS demand an explanation. It can only be that, however hazy he may be on details, his conviction is firm, his team determined to 'roll back the state' and complete the work Margaret Thatcher began in the 1980s. When critics observed that Lansley could have secured most of his ends incrementally by inserting GPs into the primary care trusts and building up commissioning gradually, they missed the point. His plan is designed simultaneously to open tens of billions' worth of NHS work to private enterprise and to dismantle this monument to postwar socialism; Tory protestations of affection for the NHS have always been through gritted teeth. Nick Timmins even entitled his study of the plan for the Institute for Government 'Never Again', to signify Lansley's determination to make his market reforms permanent.

The full extent of what is planned was revealed by Mark Britnell, a Cameron intimate and former NHS manager who heads health at KPMG. Unguarded in New York, he urged private equity investors to swoop. 'The NHS will be shown no mercy,' he said. 'In future the NHS will be a state insurance provider, not a state deliverer.'[31] The NHS will, at best, become a kitemark, a shell within which competitive forces are played out as more patients rely on private insurance for top-ups and co-payments, leading towards the American way.

There's the dogma. The disarray follows from Tory impatience for 'reform' at a time when healthcare is under severe financial constraint. Lansley's counter-reformation is consuming £2 billion in administration, changing jobs, badges and titles. After a decade of rapid growth in spending, Labour had applied the brakes and obliged the NHS to cut £20 billion from the cost of its everyday functioning, the money to be redirected to meet the ever-rising expense of healthcare for an ageing population. As the bills for ageing and new drugs mount, the NHS needs an extra 2 per cent added to its annual budget above general inflation just for services to stand still. Cameron's face had been plastered on election posters promising not to cut NHS spending;

the Coalition Agreement guaranteed a real terms increase in each year of the parliament.

But overall health spending is at best flat, or dropping slightly, so the gap between that promised rise and the 2 per cent the NHS needs to stand still is wide, causing lengthening waiting lists for operations and a spate of clinic closures.

Both Thatcher in 1989 and Blair in 1998 faced winter hospital crises when they let the NHS budget fall below that critical 2 per cent increase. By 2015 health spending will be the same in real terms as in 2010, five years over which demand for care for older people is accelerating and councils are slicing into budgets for social care, knocking costs back into hospitals.

The NHS had been a Labour success. By 2010 pollsters awarded it the highest levels of public satisfaction they had ever recorded. Spending had doubled over the 13 years; NHS waiting lists for surgery had vanished; doctor numbers increased by two-thirds, nurses by a third. Of course arguments raged over the effectiveness of the increases; healthcare productivity is notoriously hard to measure. The Tories attacked NHS 'bureaucracy' but though manager numbers had risen, they were still only 3.4 per cent of NHS staff, much lower than in insurance-based systems in other countries.

Because the NHS was so popular, Cameron's PR skills were deployed. The cameras were given discreet glimpses of his disabled child. He and Lansley joined the picket line outside Chase Farm hospital in Enfield, vowing no hospital closures on their watch. Once elected, the Coalition Agreement also seemed to reiterate the Tories' stated opposition to any turbulent new NHS reform.

So far so expedient. But then the published programme for government turned the language upside down, majoring on markets, competition and choice. Once safely in office,

Lansley introduced the voluminous Health and Social Care Bill, ready-made and pre-planned. Despite vicissitudes, several uncharacteristically rowdy Lords rebellions, a brief uprising by Liberal Democrat conference delegates leading to a pause and a review, it has now become law. With minor amendments, its essence remains the intention to open every particle of the NHS to competition from bidders who, in most cases, will be profit-making companies. Monitor, previously the overseer of NHS Foundation Trusts, was reshaped to crack the whip on competition. It is chaired by Patrick Carter, whose day job – conveniently – is running a private health company.[32] Labour originally appointed him and, as Cameron often said with glee, it had already pushed the door ajar. Blair introduced private surgery centres to ginger up hospital consultants suspected of keeping long waiting lists deliberately to boost their private practice and their waiting lists fell in consequence. Blair had also forced through partly independent foundation trusts to run hospitals, ambulances and mental health. But now they too are being forced to let private firms compete for their services. Nothing Labour did prefigured this all-out assault on the coherence of the NHS. Somehow the magic of competition is expected to iron out the duplications it invites. Lansley does not explain what happens when all providers choose to drop an unprofitable area of work. Labour set a cap of around 2 per cent on what NHS hospitals could sell in the private market, but now hospitals can use up to 49 per cent of their beds, scans or services to make money from private patients. If NHS beds and operating theatres are full of paying patients, NHS patients face longer waits. Those who can afford it may go private and the NHS will eventually become a residual service for the poor. When Labour cut waiting times to near zero, the number of people paying to go private fell steeply and the private sector fretted over its empty beds.

THE ULTIMATE PRIVATIZATION

This likely trajectory has been hidden from public view. Instead, Lansley claimed he was enfranchising GPs as 'commissioners' and holders of the NHS purse. The cosy image of family doctors choosing personal services for each patient seduced many journalists, who obligingly called it a 'bill that puts GPs in control of the NHS'. It does not, which is why the Royal College of General Practitioners was among its first and most vociferous opponents. What replaces Primary Care Trusts are Care Commissioning Groups (CCGs), in most areas only nominally run by GPs who are often reluctant to do more than token managerial work. The 212 CCGs are fifty more in number than the old PCTs, creating an increase in what Lansley sneered at as 'bureaucracy'. Some are expected to be amalgamated, probably returning eventually to the same number as PCTs in a circular disorganization that saw some of the best managers and scarce finance directors depart the NHS in despair.

Many GPs do not want to run a market: they were trained to care for patients. But GPs are a mixed lot and the entrepreneurs among them are setting up their own clinics and specialist arms, to which patients may be referred without realizing their doctors have a stake in the profits. Virgin Care has partnerships with the GPs in twenty-five CCGs. In Bath and North East Somerset CCG all six GPs are part of a Virgin Care partnership providing outside clinics for fractures and deep vein thrombosis that the GPs may refer patients to: Virgin Care says it has 'procedures in place to manage conflicts of interest'. But other countries, even the US, ban such crossovers. A GP cheerleader for the reforms in Surrey has already been caught dumping scores of high-cost frail 'unprofitable' patients from his list, a portent of markets to come. These are just the first tastes of NHS commercialization.

One reason GPs voted so overwhelmingly against the NHS bill when asked by their Royal College, was their concern that far from gaining extra control over what services to buy for their patients, the reality is that financial control, accountability and power is often elsewhere, yet blame for any cuts and rationing rests with them. Whitehall's understandable fear of handing over the bulk of the NHS budget to amateur doctor-managers means what GPs do in their surgeries is being second-guessed as the CCGs develop as a new bureaucratic tier. When GPs refer patients to hospital consultants, the CCG may intervene, applying its own rationing criteria and increasingly its obligation to look for private suppliers of healthcare. The Lansley Act specifically instructs CCGs to put competitiveness first, meaning they must always choose the Most Economically Advantageous Tender (MEAT): that means the cheapest. Although in theory treatments are costed according to an approved NHS tariff, big firms may at first bid low as a way of undercutting NHS hospitals and clinics, only to put prices up later when they dominate the market and have driven chunks of the NHS to the wall. So much for the idea of patient choice: commissioning the most cost-effective will often mean no choice, if the patient or the GP who favours their local NHS hospital finds it has been closed down.

The control tower of the new system is the National Commissioning Board (NCB) with 3,500 staff. In a remarkable act of political hara-kiri – but consonant with his faith in markets – Lansley had wanted to shed altogether the legal responsibility of the Secretary of State to ensure that healthcare is provided for all. But MPs were never going to leave themselves open to complaints by constituents without being able to summon the responsible minister to reply in the Commons, and he was thwarted.

Instead of clear responsibility, Lansley has spawned a spaghetti organogram. A new regional apparatus under the NCB will force the pace on competition and prevent GPs commissioning from tried and trusted NHS providers. Cunningly, the plan is to privatize these regional satraps too, probably outsourcing them to consultancies such as PricewaterhouseCoopers. Its rival KPMG supplied several of Cameron's ideological storm troopers, among them Paul Kirby, a Number Ten policy adviser, and Britnell himself. The American giant McKinsey has already penetrated the structure, a commercializing woodworm.

Elastoplast has had to be applied to cover trips and falls, even before the system is up and running. Two of the prototype regions, Mercia and Devon and Cornwall, have already collapsed under the weight of complexity. Some 90,000 NHS staff are being required to reapply for their old jobs under a new name, perhaps now outside the NHS. If the Lansley plan holds, they will be joined by tens of thousands more, for whom the big question will be whether their terms and conditions are protected under transfer rules. In speeches on the Big Society Cameron talked up 'social enterprise', exemplified by Central Surrey Health, a group of community nurses who set up their own company to bid for NHS work, and to whom he personally gave a Big Society award. Shortly afterwards they were passed over in competitive bidding in favour of Assura private health, an arm of the Virgin empire.

Such private companies won't be keen on collaboration and will want to keep their data tight. So pathways for stroke or cancer treatment, painstakingly set up over the last few years to bring different hospitals to work together, run the risk of dislocation. In Nottingham some thirty separate physiotherapy services are now offering NHS services. Hospital consultants, used to working closely with trusted physiotherapists, find their patients may be despatched anywhere, the cheaper the service the more attractive. Providers all have to register with the Care Quality Commission, but its budget has been cut by a third, and it is already behind on a workload swollen by new clinics, services and care homes.

The mantra of patient choice implies patients ought to have leverage over the CCGs but Lansley has instead created a cat's cradle of overlapping organizations – forgetting his boasted intolerance of bureaucracy. His promise to patients was 'no decision about me without me'; it is going to be hard to spot patient power in the new set-up. A new committee called Healthwatch England, dubiously independent and certainly not elected, will oversee local healthwatch committees to champion patients' interests; their budgets will be tiny and their only power is to issue reports and make recommendations to CCGs and councils. To add to the complexity, councils will commission the healthwatch committees and also set up new Health and Wellbeing Boards, as part of their assumption of responsibility for public health, previously part of the NHS. The Liberal Democrats wanted to bring democratic accountability to the NHS, but this salad is as far as they got.

Looking ahead to April 2013 when CCGs assume their final legal powers, NHS managers are mighty fearful, yet struggle to keep the show on the road. Mike Farrar, head of the NHS Confederation, warns that the NHS is 'a super-tanker heading for an iceberg'. British Social Attitudes reports the fastest ever fall in public approval for the NHS, from 70 per cent to 58 per cent in one year. Cameron knew that securing public trust for his custodianship of the NHS was his route to power: how apt if his betrayal of that trust helps cause his downfall.

Stakes are high. Fragmentation may precipitate financial crises. Whitehall used to transfer money between trusts to stop services falling over. Now the Lansley scheme says hospitals are to go bust: the market will decide. Either United Healthcare or other firms will step in or failing units will merge if any successful NHS services are willing to shoulder their losses. Lansley is desperate that decisions are made locally and cannot be attributed to him. But closure is often necessary, justified by changes in medical technology and the need to concentrate expertise. The government inherited plans to close some sixty hospitals or units on the basis of long-standing plans so as to group specialisms into centres of excellence and to close sub-standard A&E and maternity units. In office they have procrastinated: they presume the market will do the job for them, though that would be random and may lead to the wrong closures. Meanwhile, MPs, including from their own side, will fight any unpopular change. In May 2012 the Foreign Secretary led a march of 4,000 constituents against the downgrading of maternity and paediatric services in Northallerton. There is more trouble of this kind ahead. Coalition MPs live in dread of catching Kidderminster syndrome, first case in 2001, when a doctor campaigning to keep open a local hospital unseated a Worcestershire MP. When the Tories in Totnes opened candidate selection to all residents in an open primary they chose a Devon GP, Sarah Wollaston, who subsequently became a devastating critic of her own government's health legislation, 'throwing a hand grenade into the NHS', she said. No more open primaries have been held since.

CHAPTER 7

No pinch for pensioners

In ageing Britain all governments need a 'policy for the old'; they differ in how joined up it is, and how fairly it considers the interests of rich and poor and today and tomorrow. Cameron did not absorb the message of a distinctly un-Tory book, *The Pinch* by his clever minister, David Willetts, which appeared just as they took office: it deplored how the generation now retiring had sucked up money in generous pension pots and accumulated wealth from phenomenal house price rises, squeezing the living standards of their children and grandchildren, keeping the young off the housing ladder.[33] Tory policy, however, put political expediency before intergenerational justice. Cameron treated pensioners with kid gloves and he was as unlikely to tackle retired fat cats' accretion of wealth as he was to challenge the rest of the rich. Pensioners vote more than any other group, and they tend towards the right.

The IFS estimates that spending and benefit cuts will hit the incomes of mothers and children a lot harder than pensioners.

NO PINCH FOR PENSIONERS

The intention was to make sure they were protected, so they alone face no cut in council tax benefit. That's what made Osborne's 2012 budget so surprising. He didn't announce his move directly, hoping it would slip by in the budget red book undetected by the press. But £323 a year would be taken from the special tax dispensation pensioners enjoy on incomes up to £26,000, which means hitting middling rather than rich pensioners. A noisy protest ensued but despite retreat on so many measures, this granny tax was not U-turned. It was a reasonable anomaly to iron out, but since the government went to such pains and such expense to protect pensioners, it was politically incompetent to allow such bad publicity over one relatively minor claw-back of a pensioner benefit.

The tabloids that shrieked against tax on behalf of these comparatively well-off pensioners were, as ever, inconsistent. When Iain Duncan Smith, the Work and Pensions Secretary, thrashing about under threat of having to make an extra £10 billion cuts, argued for means-testing supplements paid to all pensioners, such as the winter fuel allowance, free bus passes and free television licences for the over-75s, the *Sun* backed him with a curious campaign in support of cutting them. Internal battles raged over the proposal, but on this Cameron is too PR savvy not to fear the damage from taking on the pensioner lobby. The perk that would yield most is free pensioner prescriptions, and he is not going to touch that.

It was safer to turn the attack on public sector pensions. Osborne and Maude announced peremptorily that these would be cut by £2.8 billion and state employees must contribute 50 per cent more, without waiting for the review they asked Labour ex-minister John Hutton to write. In addition, the inflation price index for both existing and future public pensioners was to be switched, slicing at least a fifth off the value of their pension every succeeding decade. After 1979, Thatcher had provoked, confronted, defeated and then defanged the unions. Hawks in the Cameron camp yearned to reprise her triumph and seemed, in November 2011, to have provoked it with a one-day public sector strike. But despite a fleeting echo of the 1970s, the unions lacked leverage. Public opinion warmed to the government's argument that public pensions were on average twice as generous as the private sector's. That was no surprise since two-thirds of private employees have no pension at all from their employers. But people were also incensed by FTSE 100 excess and Hutton's measured report reminded them that if 78,000 out of 4 million retired public pensioners did have pensions above the average wage, the average male public sector pension was just £4,000 a year and a woman's £2,800. Evidence from the NAO and the OBR said firmly that future pension commitments, already adjusted down by Labour, were affordable. Government negotiators became more reasonable. By June 2012 1.1 million council workers quietly settled on far better terms than those so aggressively hurled at them by Maude. In the end, only the top 10 per cent of civil servants had their contributions increased, with 90 per cent paying no extra, but seeing their retirement age rise. The strife is not over. Teachers and the police are in dispute. In June 2012 doctors voted for the first time in three decades to take a day of action to defend their position; if consultants under 50 work to 68, that still allows them to earn a handsome £68,000 pension. Doctors risked squandering public support for the more important battles to come over the dismantling of the NHS.

Cameron wavered, instinctively non-interventionist, but he was urged on all sides to prevent a future when large numbers of private sector employees faced retirement with no pensions. So he kept in place NEST, the National Employment Savings Trust invented by Labour, which will automatically enrol staff with no company pension, an estimated 4 to 7 million people. Employers pay 3 per cent, employees 4 per cent and the state adds 1 per cent tax relief. But membership is not compulsory and the low-paid may opt out; for those who can't afford to save, there's a straitened old age ahead.

For some the crisis is already here when it comes to paying for care. Families indignantly discover elderly parents have to sell their homes and use their savings to cover the cost of care. In an epic example of market failure there is no effective insurance on offer, either. Local authority cuts have fallen hard on the frail elderly, requiring them to contribute ever more. Many councils now only offer care in their own homes for those with 'critical' needs, means-tested to those with savings under £23,250. Many might be looked after better in residential care, but councils are unwilling to pay the high cost except in the last months of life. So the care divide between the well off who can afford to pay and the rest has grown. Short fifteen-minute visits to wash and feed patients by rushed home carers working for agencies, low paid, have become standard.

Having walked out of cross-party talks on the future funding of care before the election, and ignoring the reams of analysis on offer, the government chose to reinvent the wheel. The academic Andrew Dilnot, former head of the IFS, was commissioned to report, adding to the many similar reports gathering dust on Whitehall shelves over the decades. Dilnot proposed everyone should pay a sum of £30,000–£50,000 on retirement, either in cash or as a lien on their property after their death. (The state would pay for those with no assets.) That would secure free care and protect the property for the relatively small numbers needing expensive residential care. To set this up, the government would have to contribute £1.7 billion. The government delayed its response till July 2012. Its white paper airily agreed with the principle but procrastinated on costs. As things stand, another five years will have passed before what is simultaneously a national need and a household emergency is addressed, political cowardice matching public refusal to think clearly about property, inheritance and fairness.

Dilnot's proposal only finds a fairer way to pay for today's inadequate levels of care. A fresh crisis is brewing as care-home owners increasingly refuse to take in state-funded residents, as what councils will pay no longer covers costs. Previous governments avoided a subject bristling with difficulties, and Cameron will also try to duck it. If he has the nerve to implement Dilnot he will do better than Labour, but if not, disarray is turning to crisis on his watch as the Care Quality Commission finds a growing proportion of care homes falling short in standards, after his deepening cuts to all services for the old.

CHAPTER 8

The unkindest cuts

Pensions aside, for Tories the easiest cuts are those to support for households on low income. This is the underbelly of the welfare state. Labour had been relatively generous to the poor – working-age childless people excepted. After thirteen years voters were suspicious of a growing bill, even though it was Labour's tax credits to low-income households *in work* that had swollen it. *British Social Attitudes* shows how opinion hardens against benefit claimants during Labour rule, but hearts soften again after Tory governments turn the screw. The tightening now going on is 'without historical or international precedence', the usually measured IFS noted. One certain effect, they said, is to increase child poverty.

Cameron is not a details man, so he allowed traditional negotiations on spending between the Treasury and each separate Whitehall department to carry on beneath his radar. Jonathan Portes of the NIESR says the government had 'an almost complete lack of attention to cross-cutting issues'. That meant cuts made by councils and by each Whitehall department 'combine to produce disproportionate impacts on vulnerable groups'.[34] The same households were often hit over and over again, while others were virtually untouched.

Austerity involved cutting the deficit primarily by attacking public spending, not by raising funds through taxes. A second step was weighting the spending cuts on social security rather than the public services enjoyed in middle England. Duncan Smith signed up to a cut of £18 billion from the Department for Work and Pensions (DWP) budget and the Treasury expects at least half as much again. A third move was to separate deserving welfare clients (pensioners, mostly) from the undeserving – as this moralizing government considers them. These are large families, poor households audaciously living in rich areas, working-age but workless families, regardless of how long the local list of applicants for available jobs might be. Even the disabled are not spared deep cuts in support.

A fourth step is to clothe welfare cuts in the mantle of administrative reform. This allows Duncan Smith to say, don't worry about reduced benefits, for tomorrow comes Universal Credit. Everyone, in work or out of work, gets a new cash benefit if their income falls below a threshold and if they work to increase their income the system will smoothly adjust, giving them an incentive to seek employment rather than, as now, he claimed, facing a steep loss in welfare payments on taking a job. That, at least, is his claim, though Labour's working tax credits had already ensured work paid for almost all. But making his new system work depends on marrying HMRC and DWP computers and diverting billions of the planned savings from welfare cuts to pay for the new system. Logically that would precipitate more cuts to compensate. In the summer of 2012, the Treasury and DWP were locked in brutal confrontation over where, when and how.

Why Cameron should entrust the cutting and reshaping of welfare to Duncan Smith needs explaining. This, after all, is the right-winger who undermined the Major government and then himself led the Tory Party, briefly and disastrously. But he has since reinvented himself as the Tory champion of social justice, setting up a think-tank and temporarily convincing community activists on notorious Glasgow housing estates of his Roman Catholic concern for the destitute. For Duncan Smith social justice – hence his utility to Cameron – is not about money or benefits but moral rearmament, better parenting, 'just say no' solutions to drug addiction.

Personal relations between prime minister and sainted minister are not good, so it's unclear how far Cameron knows what Duncan Smith is doing. With the Treasury, DWP has connived a permanent annual reduction in the real value of benefits. This involves an apparently innocuous switch from uprating benefits and some tax thresholds by the retail price index (RPI) measure of inflation to the lower consumer price index (CPI), a ploy invisible to the naked eye of most claimants and commentators, though its effects grow over the years. That sleight of hand means the real value of benefits will shrink by some 10 per cent every decade, the poor forever falling further behind. But the favoured dependents, pensioners, are carefully protected and a 'triple lock' on the basic state pension guarantees it will rise by the higher of RPI inflation, average earnings growth, or 2.5 per cent. The resources available to welfare claimants will over time diverge further and further from the mainstream – a result for a government that never believed in relative poverty.

Labour began contracting out what Jobcentres do to help

the unemployed back into jobs or training. The Cameron government ploughed full speed ahead. Its Work Programme will permanently demolish the state's capacity to get people into employment – a cornerstone of social policy since Lloyd George – handing most of what Jobcentres do to profit-making companies. The success of Work Programme contractors depends on the availability of jobs: Duncan Smith has refused to publish their early results, but experts expect them to fall far short of the targets set. Analysts have been puzzling over why this longest recession has not pushed jobless totals up to the extent many feared. Figures have fluctuated, so June 2012 suddenly showed an upward blip where private sector jobs were being created at twice the rate public sector jobs were being lost, a well-nigh perfect result for the Cameron–Osborne plan, but hard to explain or sustain when growth was flat or negative. Long-term unemployment is rising, with half a million people out of work for more than a year. In May 2012, the number of full-time jobs was still falling: it was part-time work that had increased. In an exceptional piece of harshness, part-timers were unaccountably picked on by the Cameron government. Some 1.4 million of them were urgently seeking full-time jobs, but if couples could not find more than 24 hours of work a week they lost their working tax credits, cutting £74 a week out of a household income of £17,000 a year. The minimum wage fell in value: although it increases to £6.08 an hour in late 2012 affecting 890,000 employees, its real worth has fallen back to what it was in 2004.

Young people are certainly feeling the impact of the recession, 20 per cent of them now without work (twice as many young black as young white men). Ministers laid into 'layabouts', echoing the tabloids, but the government has also made finding work harder. It abolished Labour's £1 billion Future Jobs Fund, which guaranteed a minimum wage job for every young person. The government claimed that many of its graduates returned to the dole but the independent NIESR said abolishing it had a lot to do with why youth unemployment had since tripled. As in many fields, the government condemned and abolished a Labour-era scheme only to have to restore something similar, but on a shoestring. Osborne's first scheme promised to exempt employers from paying any national insurance if they took on long-term unemployed people – but none did, and it failed completely. Next the government brought in its own Youth Contract, offering £2,200 to employers taking on a long-term unemployed young person. But it offers only 160,000 places, when there are more than a million unemployed young people, and its results may be no better.

Workless young people must do unpaid jobs, the government said, or they would lose benefits. Soon Tesco was using thousands on 'work experience' to stack shelves, offering them no training and no prospect of a job at the end. But the government had misjudged public attitudes: although many believed the unemployed should do something useful in exchange for their benefits, they were not in favour of them working unpaid for profit-making companies. The accusation of using slave labour was damaging to its reputation and, embarrassed, Tesco immediately offered the minimum wage and a permanent job to anyone who graduated from a six-week placement. It emerged a security company had bussed in unemployed people to act as unpaid stewards during the Jubilee festivities, forcing them to sleep under a bridge in the rain for the night. A4e, one of the biggest companies brought in under the Work Programme, was found to have used unemployed people to work in its own offices at cut rates, pocketing the fee they received for getting them off the dole. Police were called to investigate allegations of fraud within the company and its chairman Emma Harrison was forced to resign as an adviser to Cameron in February 2012 in the face of controversy over how much she had made from state contracts.

The scandal called into question the basis of the Work Programme. Ministers claimed they had protected the public purse by not paying contractors such as A4e till they found clients work; but without an army of inspectors, how would they know the jobs were real? To soften up opinion, ministers promised that charities would take the lion's share of the work. But the voluntary sector was cast aside when all but two of the big Work Programme contracts were let to giants such as Serco. Their eye on profit margins, the risk is that companies will try to pick easy cases and, having banked the higher up-front fee paid for hard cases, often park, defer or pass them on to the charities, exploiting their experience with ex-prisoners, addicts and the mentally ill.

The theory was that firms were much better at job-finding than the DWP, though the Public Accounts Committee found that in Pathways to Work, an earlier trial scheme, companies had performed worse than the civil servants. It's difficult to know, as Duncan Smith said freedom of information law did not apply to contractors, so companies' results could not be compared with the DWP itself, which is obliged to be transparent. Contractors are not going to make money effortlessly. It's tough finding jobs for hard-to-place people at a time when there are five jobless for every vacancy – fourteen in many areas. But the companies have bargaining power, and will come back to demand more money, as the DWP staff are cut. With them go the state's eyes and ears, and the means to check what a contractor is doing in comparison with the public service. The jobless come in all shapes and sizes and writing contracts comprehensive enough is hard, especially if firms want rapid rewards and are prepared to cut corners. The Work Programme may test to destruction the Letwin idea of a 'weightless state'.

Down that ideological track, why should a Tory government pay any attention to *how* people live – together, apart, with or without children? But the Tories worried about marriage and parenting. Cameron's claim they were the party of the family was reinforced before the election with domestic god pictures of him cooking porridge for the children's breakfast. He promised to be 'the most family-friendly government ever' but all his well-constructed family imagery belied his policy. To fulfil pledges on a 'more civilized work-life balance' his best offer has only been to let couples share their maternity leave. There is no sign of the right for all to ask employers for flexible working hours that Cameron had promised in 2007.

The great step backwards for families has been financial. Although the Treasury raised Child Tax Credits, which helped poorer families, Child Benefit was frozen for three years. Cameron had vowed not to means-test it but that's what will happen: families are losing the benefit when a single earner's income pushes into the 40 per cent tax bracket.

Here was a case study in Cameron's style of policy-making. Removing Child Benefit from the better off was to be proof that the government was acting fairly and besides it would save £2.4 billion. Politically, Cameron was on the button, as focus groups showed people no longer thought the top 10 per cent of earners needed or deserved Child Benefit. The move was an attack on universalism, the welfare state principle that benefits are for everyone, regardless of circumstances; if he succeeded with benefits, then health or schooling might be next. But selectivity brought with it complex questions about exactly where means tests should kick in. As so often Cameron's attitude seemed to be that if the headline worked politically, the administrative details could take care of themselves, and he shrugged off warnings. From the day the cut was announced, alarm bells rang. A single-income family on £42,474 lost its entire Child Benefit, the whole £1,750 for two children, a hefty all-or-nothing penalty if your boss gave you even a £1 pay rise. Yet why should two earners on £41,000 each remain entitled to the whole sum? Vestigial Toryism was offended: shouldn't stay-at-home wives be supported? That was the point of the 'marriage bonus', which Tory traditionalists kept saying they wanted to see in the tax system. What's more, the Child Benefit change breached the principle of separate taxation for men and women, and an additional half-million households would have to fill out tax forms.

The political storm raged and at the last possible moment before the cut was to be brought in, the Treasury ensured those earning between £50,000 and £60,000 lost benefit less precipitously. This reduces savings from the change yet leaves in place a cliff-edge over which many families still lose 50 pence for each extra pound they earn. Expect a reaction in January 2013, when the changes take hold.

Family friendliness didn't obviously characterize Cameron's other measures. He abandoned the Child Trust Fund, Labour's effort to endow all children at 18 with a nest egg to contribute to the cost of education or a home down-payment. The 2010 budget abolished a set of grants and credits for pregnant women and those with very young children. Sure Start children's centres were thrown on the tender mercies of cash-strapped councils: Tory counties and boroughs had never liked them and now got their chance to close or shrivel many of them. Labour's scheme of credits to pay for childcare was cut, forcing families to spend more on nurseries where costs were rising faster than inflation. Childcare in Britain is already the most expensive in the OECD, and for families this cut tips the balance against low-earning mothers working outside the home – not exactly a pro-growth policy.

As for helping mothers gain financial support from the fathers of their children – a laudable pro-family and cost-saving effort, you might think – policy was unintelligible. Invented by the Major government, the Child Support Agency, now the Child Maintenance and Enforcement Commission, had struggled; won't-pay fathers still owe a backlog of £3.7 billion. Oddly, this quango was not quite culled. Instead mothers are to be deterred from using it by making them pay a sizeable commission on every penny the agency collects for them from absent fathers. Legal aid to pay for court action on parental support and access to children was also removed.

If Cameron was friendlier to fathers (the errant kind) than mothers, he had no time for poor families who were targeted in what felt like a national smear campaign, especially against those with three or more children. While claiming education, good parenting and solid families were the best cure for poverty, in the worst cases government policies were set to tear poor children away from friends, grandparents, school and the social supports that help keep households together, sending them sometimes hundreds of miles away. But the politics were brilliant.

No working-age family, said Osborne in his first budget, could in future draw more in benefits than the average household receives in income, fixing the cap at £26,000. He grabbed the headlines. Around 67,000 households in Great Britain would be hit, cutting their entitlement by an average of £83 per week. But in what way had they offended? Two-thirds of those getting anywhere near £26,000 or £500 a week in benefits had three or more children and over half lived in London, where high housing costs meant most of that money paid the rent on often squalid homes. The aim, presumably, was to force them to move and get jobs or, as the IFS delicately put it, the 'third possible form of behavioural response is in lowering fertility rates'. Duncan Smith, unlike the pope, did not appear keen on procreation.

The cap sounded reasonable, certainly to the half of the population earning less than £26,000. By including their high rents in the cap, the government cleverly made poor families look as if they were living the life of Riley. But applying it in the South East could leave households with three children with £100 a week or less to live on, after paying rent on a three-bed flat. Ministers illustrated the necessity of this cut with stories from the *Daily Mail* and the *Sun* about workless Somali or Roma families living in mansions in Kensington, making rare cases sound typical. The promise to exempt those on Disability Living Allowance from the cap was deceptive, as in 2013 two-thirds of the disabled will be taken off this benefit.

If the cap in itself affects relatively few, behind it looms profound state-enforced social change. Excluding pensioners and the disabled, half the households getting Housing Benefit are in work. Now it too was to be capped, £250 a week for a flat, £420 a week for a four-bed home. If those sums sounded generous in Huddersfield, they do not go far in Haringey. The consequences will take time to play out, as the cap applies when tenancies come up for renewal. But private rented turnover is high and families are already being forced out of more affluent boroughs in what feels like class clearance. Ministers don't demur: if you can't afford to live here, move out. So much for the community cohesion on which the theory of Cameron's Big Society depends.

To be officially homeless, families have to wait for the bailiffs literally to push them out on the pavement, then council obligations kick in. London councils, anticipating they will have large numbers on their hands, are looking at accommodation as far away as Stoke-on-Trent and Hull, where property is vacant because jobs are scarce. Suddenly place counts for nothing. The basis of social housing is changing as new council and housing association tenancies are now to last only five years. With rents pushed up to 80 per cent of the market level, social housing will be unaffordable in the South East for anyone on the minimum wage.

The policy may cause an evacuation as large as the settlements of hundreds of thousands of Londoners into New Towns in the 1940s and 1950s. That offered gleaming new homes; this is a vindictive class clearance, unrelated to any strategic thinking about employment, transport or housing supply. The same empiricism applies to the benefit changes. If families suffer, it may not matter politically since society is atomized, community groups are weak and councils are compliant or cowed.

Yet it's not clear whether ministers fully understand what they are doing. Evidence comes from the way Cameron allowed Duncan Smith to dash for the simplification of benefits that, in a complex and diverse society such as ours, is not to be had except at huge extra cost. His Universal Credit isn't. Alongside, free school meals and childcare credits will continue as separate benefits. These have to be responsive to place and changes in family circumstance, and can't easily be slotted into a single template. Simplification also turned out to mean passing the buck. Poor households used to qualify for a benefit to help pay their council tax. That has been sloughed off to councils, who can choose to pay it or not, as long as they protect pensioners. The Social Fund, which loans sums as small as £5 a day to stop people starving, disappears; instead councils will be grant-aided at less than the Social Fund's cost and left to decide if they want to support the poorest in crisis or spend the money on municipal roses.

Before, when he was a compassionate Conservative, Cameron

said he would 'never do anything to hurt disabled children', a pledge made convincing by his own family circumstances. Yet the budget for Disability Living Allowance (DLA) is being cut by 20 per cent. Available both to those in and out of work and children, this pays for day centre fees and personal assistance. Two-thirds of families with disabled children will lose, to the tune of £1,400 a year. Two out of five families with a disabled child live below the poverty line, mothers staying at home to care instead of going out to work. They will become even poorer. Some 25,000 children and young people who look after disabled parents will lose £70 a week. In addition, the government plans to reorganize how 1.7 million children with special education needs are helped: instead of the council providing, their families are given a grant to purchase services.

Some 643,000 people registered as disabled are to lose all support, including mobility allowances, saving £2 billion. Attacking payments for incapacity, the government exulted in tales of fraud, with allegedly sick claimants caught on camera water-skiing or fixing roofs, even though the government's own figures showed only 0.5 per cent of claims were fraudulent. Claims were said to have risen steeply under Labour: 'the incubation of the benefits culture was one of Labour's great sins', Duncan Smith the moralist claimed. In fact numbers on incapacity benefit and its successor, Employment Support Allowance (ESA), had been falling under Labour; claimants were already undergoing more rigorous checks on their fitness to take jobs. Numbers on DLA had risen because people were living longer with illnesses and more severely disabled and damaged premature babies were surviving to adulthood. Diabetes was disabling many more people. Mentally ill people who previously had not claimed were coming forward in greater numbers following tribunal decisions establishing their entitlement. Such social facts were conveniently ignored. Duncan Smith preferred tales of layabouts and offered sycophantic journalists his thought for the day: 'This is not an easy life any more, chum, I think you're a slacker.'

So far the public seems to agree with the sentiment. But the harshest measures have yet to be implemented and already, in a panic, Cameron himself has had to step in and deny that the cuts will apply to service personnel injured in Iraq and Afghanistan. What of disabled police officers, life-boatmen, fire fighters and other 'deserving' categories, including those disabled children he swore to protect? Scrounger headlines are easy, but administration is a headache. New tests for all those on DLA are costing £675 million. Tougher ESA tests, contracted out to private firms, are disqualifying 37 per cent of claimants. But of those who appeal, nearly four in ten get the decision overturned. Appeals tribunals are gridlocked and it can take a year to get a case heard. The Citizens Advice Bureau wants the contractor fined for every case that is overturned: working to a target to cut claimant numbers may not be just, and before long the public may think so too. Knowingly, or as a result of his wandering attention to policy, Cameron has exposed himself to the charge of loading on poor households a disproportionate and deeply unfair share of 'fiscal tightening'; the Tories, the erstwhile patriotic party, have staked Britain's reputation for decency.

But without waiting to see the effect of all these cuts already planned, he is going further still. When in trouble and flagging in the polls in summer 2012, Cameron made a sudden démarche. If cutting welfare was his one indisputably popular policy, why not promise a lot more of it? He floated a seventeen-point plan that was especially savage towards the young: under-25s would lose all housing benefit and must live at home. Many can't; and what of the new graduate from, say, Middlesbrough, setting off to rent a room in a place where there are jobs? Forget social mobility if everyone must stay where they are born. Cameron would break the link between benefits and inflation, and time-limit benefits, US style, so they run out for the long-term unemployed. Then what? He promised a tougher cap on housing benefit, cutting benefit for larger families – and, particularly harsh, cutting benefit rates in poorer areas to increase the North–South living standards divide. He was flag-waving at his own party, marking out territory to fight the next election, as the Liberal Democrats might not agree to all this, but some of this he intends to press on with now. His most popular policy may not stay so indefinitely.

CHAPTER 9

Back to the Future

Family friendliness was not for Michael Gove either. His first move was to unscrew the plaques and change the stationery so that the cuddly Department for Children, Schools and Families became the straight Department for Education (DfE). Yet the minister turned out to be no prophet of orderliness, but rather an educational anarchist happy to turn over schools – and the intellectual fate of hundreds of thousands – to experiments. His signature Free Schools were usually little more than the pet projects of cliques of parents whose interest was bound to wane once their own children had moved on. With academies and University Technical Colleges, Gove's grand ambition was shown to be nothing less than reinventing the 1944 Education Act, grammar schools and all, but with local authorities largely excluded. He would move crabwise to expand selection in secondary schools and, as he confided to the Leveson enquiry, welcome private companies in running state schools for a profit.[35]

Schools in England had improved under Labour. The percentage of pupils achieving five or more GCSEs grades A*–C had risen to a high of 79 per cent in 2010/11. The percentage gaining three or more A-level passes rose by 20 per cent between 1997 and 2005, with nearly three-quarters now staying on in education until 18. But though only 7 per cent are privately educated, the system was still dominated by payment and selection. Nearly one-third of independent school pupils and more than one-quarter of selective school pupils gained three or more As at A-Level in 2010/11, compared with only one in twelve comprehensive pupils – but at least that represented a rise from one in twenty in 1997.

Gove had free rein because education was neither a Cameron priority nor a particular interest. Education spending is to fall by over 13 per cent in real terms between 2010 and 2015, returning it as a proportion of GDP to the 4.6 per cent ratio Labour had inherited in 1997 – which Labour had pushed up to 6.4 per cent by 2009/10. Even if, buildings aside, Gove could claim spending on England's primary and secondary schools was relatively protected, spending per pupil in real terms was going to fall. The Tory experiment is about what happens to results as a consequence.

Ministers talked of concentrating spending on poor pupils, pushing up results overall. In fact Gove's structural changes pulled the system in the other direction – favouring better-off pupils in better-off schools with louder and pushier parents than poor children tend to have. Free schools were being created by parents to control access, siting them in favoured areas; the building costs siphon off money from what's left in the general investment pot. As for private schools, the government left the Charity Commission in no doubt its future was in jeopardy if it persisted in applying Labour's legislation requiring private schools to demonstrate their public benefit – an impossible task. When Gove made a keynote speech deploring the decline in social mobility, citing the heavy concentration of privately educated men and women among his Cabinet colleagues, his subtext emerged: the re-creation of selective schools, grammars or their equivalent within the state sector, to pluck brighter children from poor homes.

Among his colleagues Gove was sure-footed. But the peculiar arrogance in power that afflicted the Cameron government claimed him as its first victim. He had to backtrack after high-handedly trying to end, immediately, Labour's Building Schools for the Future programme, a £55 billion plan to rebuild or refurbish all secondary schools in England by 2023. This followed from trying to protect revenue spending on schools by offloading the cuts on investment – a recipe for trouble in later years.

Quick on the legislative draw, Gove got his Academies Act through within a couple of months, and schools responded to the bribes on offer to convert into these free-standing institutions outside the control of councils, paid for directly from Whitehall. Headteachers and governors were not ideological converts but they were pragmatic. They went where the money was and an investigation subsequently found the converting schools had been paid £120 million, even more than the formula permitted,[36] with the excess clawed back from the schools stubbornly remaining with councils.

On the face of it, Gove was merely picking up where Labour had left off. Their stated purpose had been to replace the worst schools in poor areas. Gove's academies were converted from among the best schools, which were handed more power to select and exclude. Schools that would not convert would, like Protestants under Mary Tudor, be encouraged: the entire governing body of Downhills primary in Haringey was sacked and, despite parents' expressed wishes, the school forced into academy status with new governors handpicked by the minister.

In his war on councils, Gove tore up the formula by which schools had been paid for through the town and county halls. Instead, DfE now calculates each school's funding centrally, according to a single formula. Making the announcement Gove chose not to exemplify the effects of the change perhaps because, as the IFS found, his policy results in a list of winners and losers that's hard to explain and impossible to justify: schools in Wigan, Liverpool and North East Lincolnshire will lose; those in Islington and Warwickshire will gain. In the same area secondaries will gain and primaries lose and vice versa. With one in six schools seeing funding per pupil cut by 10 per cent or more the IFS suggested that, at the very least, the changeover should be extended over a six- to ten-year period, but it is being rushed in.

The Cameron welfare reforms toughened the eligibility requirements for free school meals. But this proxy for household poverty is being used as the basis for calculating the new pupil premium: restricting it cuts the number of pupils getting the premium. Advertised as a way of targeting resources, its £2.5 billion cost met by cuts elsewhere in education, it turns out to have rotten sights, shifting money from cities to shires. Stranger still, schools are under no obligation to spend the extra on poor pupils themselves; they could use the money to repaint the head's study. That chimes with Gove's philosophy of educational atomism – individual schools going their own way – but he was also encouraging the growth of chains of schools, with linked services and central administration. According to the National College for School Leadership, by September 2012 there were likely to be forty-eight chains with at least three schools in them, some with ten or more academies, with a wide geographical spread. They feel like precursors to privatization: once the local state has been eliminated and schools come in all shapes and sizes, the door opens to private school owners. Already, some chain chieftains had acquired a taste for the finer things that educational profits can buy. No wonder the custodians of public spending started twitching. The House of Commons Public Accounts Committee said the DfE had to do a lot more work to define how funding streams would be monitored and audited, and make sure whistle-blowers were heard. 'We are alarmed by reports of worrying expenditure by some schools – for example, very high salaries being paid to senior staff in academies or excessive expense payments for governors – which could be symptomatic of more system-wide concerns such as the adequacy of governance and controls on value for money.'[37]

It isn't just accountability. Fragmentation makes it much harder to bring teachers together in schemes for professional improvement. Gove abolished the General Teaching Council, created by Labour as a way of instilling pride in teaching staff, giving them similar registration and expulsion arrangements as doctors. A leaked email from Gove's adviser Dominic Cummings blamed the teachers for dumbing down exams and said Gove should not speak to them anymore, hardly a recipe for better schooling.[38] His appointee as head of Ofsted and chief inspector, Sir Michael Wilshaw, was a successful head and tyrannous in his reflexes, saying eccentrically that heads should model themselves on Clint Eastwood. (Gove turned out to watch different movies: he withdrew Wilshaw's threat of no-notice inspections saying such interventions would turn Ofsted into Sean Connery's *Untouchables*, and he did not want that.)

Gove, the advocate of freedom, then sent a King James Bible to every school bearing his own signature, with the clear implication it should be studied, if not prayed over, and even tried to pay for the intervention with public money. Freedom was not apparently to extend to the curriculum, as Gove demanded specific changes in maths and history. But money previously dedicated to school sports was absorbed into the general grant and, on the eve of the Olympics, Sport England was reporting fewer young people involved in sports. Culture, Media and Sport Secretary Jeremy Hunt denied it was a result of moving away from a ringfenced budget.[39]

Cameron remained silent, as conflicting Tory instincts fought one another. Gove sounded elitist, focused on the better pupils, unconcerned if participation rates beyond the age of 16 fell. How did this approach (Cameron might have asked) square with the OECD saying the principal measure of a nation's growth potential is high participation in schooling and higher education? Young people who had been given an incentive to continue in education by means of the Labour-created Education Maintenance Allowance fell foul of the Gove restriction: the £30 a week received by poorest post-16 students was abruptly ended. The IFS said the allowance had encouraged students but the government preferred the evidence of tabloid stories about them using the money to buy mobile phones.

Yet, with the prime minister absent from debates, the government ostentatiously preserved from its quango cull the Office of Fair Access, which existed to widen participation in higher education. With universities and research, Cameron tried to back rival horses. One was privatization. Higher education would become a market, transforming existing public universities into private institutions and allowing new profit-making companies to grant degrees. Another was securing the UK's capacity to function as a modern economy, based on the accumulation of knowledge and research. As with pensions, David Willetts, the universities and science minister, had an unpalatable message. Keeping up in biotechnology, pharmaceuticals, materials, nanotechnology, digital, energy and low carbon technologies implied not just massive public support but active state leadership.

So how would a university market built around students choosing where they would get best value for money in teaching serve Willetts' demand for research excellence and the maintenance of at least a dozen UK universities in the world's top 100 (according to *Times Higher Education* rankings)? The government put its money where its mouth was by maintaining the £4.6 billion science budget in cash terms. But the budget for higher education, excluding research, was cut by £2.9 billion or 40 per cent. So where would the money come from to support expensive excellence as the state withdrew – from business, families, or students? Certainly the latter, as the government brings in full-cost tuition and makes going to college an encounter with prolonged indebtedness.

Labour had also tried to ride the two horses. Unwilling to back elitism and support a small number of internationally competitive universities because of what that implied for funding the rest, Labour had tried to pump in extra money by introducing variable fees for UK universities in 2006 up to a maximum of £3,000. Applications fell but the upward trend resumed and the proportion of those aged between 18 and 30 attending a higher education institution rose to 48 per cent as Labour left office, not far short of Blair's target of 50 per cent.

The Tories had derided Labour's targets, so did Cameron actually want more students? The government dodged the question by adopting full-cost upfront fees for undergraduates, a policy that had the incidental effect of destroying the Liberal Democrats' reputation for political integrity, since in the 2010 election they had so vehemently promised to vote against any increase in fees. Charging extra looks as if it will deter applications. Loans are available, to be repaid once a graduate earns more than £21,000 – up from Labour's £15,000 threshold – and now part-time students are entitled to them as well.

Was the point to concentrate the best students in elite universities (which could afford to be more generous with scholarships), and what should that imply for the lower-ranking universities, with students mainly from less well-off backgrounds? As if to mitigate the desired effect – to make higher education more elitist – the government scrambled to keep students from poorer backgrounds. A new £150 million National Scholarships Programme will be targeted at bright but poor students, offering benefits such as a free first year. Students from families with incomes of up to £25,000 are entitled to a more generous maintenance grant. Loan repayments are structured according to income earned.

Willetts insisted he was making the universities more autonomous and 'putting choice and power in the hands of students'. Raising fees gave private colleges their chance. 'This reform opens up the system. We will also allow alternative providers to access the generous system of student loans and grants'.[40] Deregulation will make it easier for new education companies to offer degrees. But so far it's a peculiar market. Ministers are determined to intervene, instructing universities on the number and type of students they can recruit: only top universities are allowed to compete to take as many as they choose, but at specified fees and as long as students have high A-level scores. The oddest ingredient of this market was that foreign students are to be excluded: though they pay high fees for which universities compete fiercely, Cameron's arbitrary pledge to cut net immigration meant restricting their visas.

There, yet again, is an example of Cameron's contrary impulses. He has allowed Gove to set off back to the future, as if the English school system of the twenty-first century looked like 1955's. But 'system' is a misnomer. Where did anarchist free schools fit when Gove was dictating the curriculum, imagining himself a Napoleonic education director who could pick up his watch and say, 'It is 11 o'clock and at this moment, across France, all pupils are reciting the future subjunctive of the verb *être*.' So Cameron's policy for education split. From 5 to 16, Gove was busy separating the sheep from the goats, pushing the poor and less bright students into the lower tier, talking up standards. From 18, the elements of mass higher education were left in place, and new fly-by-night operators being encouraged to offer cheaper degrees. Education was not only increasingly riven, the Cameron approach was also to downgrade its budget: it did not sound like a basis for the knowledge economy.

CHAPTER 10

Omnishambles

Behind the confusion on education lies deeper doubt about the purposes of this government. To cut the public sector, expand the space in which business can make profit – these goals only took it so far. What kind of Britain did Cameron want to create? No answer comes from his government's hesitations, false starts and ineffectiveness, for example over Europe. Whatever his domestic disarray, abroad he often seemed merely hapless, as when at the G20 summit in the US in June 2012 he let himself be waylaid in the corridors by the Argentine president seeking vengeance for the Falklands war.[41]

All governments face wicked issues, old intractables for which, because no single easy or politically palatable solution exists, successive cabinets fail to resolve. These include lack of housing, the dearth of high-quality job training and sluggish productivity, the widening North–South divide and low-calibre, grotesquely rewarded company boardrooms. But top of the list is immigration and here Cameron had over-promised, pledging to cut net immigration from 'hundreds of thousands to tens of thousands'. Blaming welfare for stopping British people taking the slots immigrants then claimed, he had to reckon with substantial increases in immigration on his watch, despite his policies and cuts. Business did not agree and clamping down on visas caused uproar in boardrooms, whose ideas about markets were apparently much more expansive than the government's.

But how to staunch the flow? To get into the UK in future, the Tories said, non-EU migrants will have to be very well off and family members will have to pass language tests. All that depends on effective border controls, but the government decided to get rid of 880 UK Border Agency staff, with another 1,550 posts to go by 2014. Immigration puts to the test the faith of those true believers who want to shrink the state. On the back foot, immigration minister Damian Green said the size of his staff doesn't matter, it's all about how staff are deployed.[42] Brodie Clark, the official in charge, thought this meant he had managerial discretion and so he deployed his fewer staff as best he could, to make fewer but more selective checks at airports. But when his laxer regime burst out into the press, he was fired without a hearing by the Home Secretary, for which he won compensation in an out-of-court settlement. Theresa May's knee-jerk response to bad headlines was to promise thorough checks on everyone, but that led to worse problems as four-hour queues built up at passport control. Airline chiefs lambasted the government. They should have said what was obvious: you could not cut immigration officials, catch more illegals, check every arrival thoroughly and still keep traffic flowing.

Most migrants came legally from other European Union countries. Business wanted them; Tory MPs, mindful of the success of the United Kingdom Independence Party, were becoming more overtly antagonistic to the EU. The debt crisis in the Eurozone was posing aching questions about EU institutions and purposes. This could have been Cameron's moment, seizing the day with his version of the UK's future or finding allies for his version of EU restructuring. He built no phalanx of EU friends. Instead, Cameron and Osborne simultaneously congratulated themselves for not being in the Eurozone, then urged closer integration of Eurozone countries and next blamed the Eurozone for the UK's economic ills. It made neither economic nor political sense.

Europe dominates Cameron's era, more even than under Major, but no coherent UK response has met the unfolding of great events: the collapse of the Euro as a grand project, Germany's hesitant self-discovery as Europe's hegemonic power and the EU's arrival at a crossroads, one track leading to dismemberment and autarky. Where was the UK? Cameron and Foreign Secretary William Hague, a proven dogmatist from his days as party leader, now had to turn his own old slogan 'Britain in Europe not run by Europe' into a working diplomatic stance. But at crunch points, for example the December 2011 summit on the Eurozone fiscal pact, Cameron was merely petulant, and petty – at first refusing but then conceding European Union mechanisms could be used for Eurozone purposes. The UK geopolitical vision narrowed to what City bosses demanded. Vetoing a new treaty, Cameron failed in his own terms to come up with an alternative model: the logic of the UK position was a multi-speed EU, or UK withdrawal, but neither was expressed as saleable policies. The summit showed just how isolated the UK was, even from the one EU leader with whom Cameron had established some rapport, the French president Nicolas Sarkozy – who dismissed Cameron's demands for multiple opt-outs as unacceptable. Cameron's ineptitude was shown only months later when, in a naïve attempt to recover his relationship with Sarkozy, he deliberately snubbed the man who then went on to defeat Sarkozy for the French presidency, François Hollande, embittering a potential diplomatic ally.

Cameron's brief foray with President Sarkozy into military action to protect Libya's insurgents was typical – unstrategic, both in the sense that it neither led to a deepening of relations with France (over defence for example) nor connected with any wider UK position on the Arab Spring or the Middle East (where Cameron led a trade delegation to sell arms to regimes not so dissimilar from Gaddafi's).

As Harold Macmillan warned, events derail you. No cabinet is immune and smoke billowing into a night sky during the riots of August 2011 also choked ministers. It was partly their dilatory response but also that after initial indignation, public opinion linked the violence to deep cuts in the support of young people, 45 per cent of whom were jobless in places where riots first flared. Cameron's Tory instincts said punish; his critics said training and employment: because his austerity ruled out both extra prisons and extra support, Cameron was tongue-tied.

His government specialized in self-harm and unforced errors, headline announcements that had to be rapidly rescinded and policies they failed to road test.

Free school milk for under-fives was abolished, then restored amid memories of Thatcher the milk-snatcher and now priced at an unaffordable £1 a mini-bottle. NHS Direct was abolished, then hastily restored under a new name, cheaper and staffed by non-medical people. Rape suspects were to get anonymity, until outraged women's groups forced a retreat. A promised military covenant enshrining the rights of service personnel was dropped from the Armed Forces bill. The Financial Inclusion Fund gave advice to vulnerable debtors. It was axed, then after protests a new scheme was hastily devised. A promise to ban circus animals became a softening of licensing conditions. A 50 per cent discount on sentences for people entering guilty pleas was abandoned, and more reverses followed over funding of the BBC Arabic Service, the coast guard, youth justice, tax relief on video games, aircraft carriers, secret courts and the date of a Scottish referendum. May 2012 saw four U-turns in a row, the pasty tax, VAT on static caravans and Osborne in retreat after massed ranks of charities rebelled at his cap on tax relief for big donations. The same week birds of prey won a reprieve: landowners protecting pheasant shoots – an expanding sector of the modern British economy – were promised a licence to destroy buzzard nests but the outcry from bird lovers put paid to that.

All governments prevaricate, change their minds and run scared of lobbies. But the Cameron style was dilettante. Public power, he seemed to believe, was there to be filched, or subverted for the benefit of the friends with whom you had country suppers, from the land-owning pheasant killers to emissaries from the court of Rupert Murdoch. Murdoch's bloated power over politicians and the arrogance of his editors was a scandal waiting to break; appointing the Murdoch apparatchik Andy Coulson as his communications director was hubristic. The *Guardian*'s persistence in investigating phone hacking by the *News of the World* forced Cameron to let him go, and then set up a judicial inquiry that became a running nightmare of embarrassment and ministerial squirming. Kowtowing to Murdoch & Son was a Labour failing too, but no one before had been so attentive to their private commercial interests. With Culture Secretary Jeremy Hunt in his back pocket and Cameron dangling on the end of James Murdoch's phone line, Murdoch Sr came within an inch of acquiring a media dominance in Britain that would have stifled all competition within a few years and led to the death of the BBC.

Civil servants say to us, how can you accuse Cameron of

purposefulness? He leaves departments uncoordinated and ministers at cross purposes, a prime minister too indolent to carry through conspiracy against the state. To which the response must be, there is an element of method in his insouciance. Civil servants are losing their jobs and their influence. The great project marches on. Whatever other disarray, this government is not for turning on cutting public spending, despite its economic effects on demand and growth.

CHAPTER 11

Half-time score

By half-time, spectators round the political stadium expected the worst to be over. The announced tactic had been to front-load spending cuts, get past the necessary pain of tax increases and give Team Tory its run-in to the next election. Growth would be well established and Osborne would scatter feel-good tax giveaways ahead of the polls. It's not going to happen. The timetable has slipped badly, so that the structural deficit in the public finances cannot be eliminated until 2016–17, and that's optimistic. Tax handouts now could only be purchased by yet more searing cuts to public services or to welfare spending.

But if Osborne lost the battle, Cameron may yet have won a war. Osborne's figures are badly awry: in 2010 he said growth at half-time would be 2.5 per cent. In April 2012 it was negative, at − 0.3 per cent, the economy in double-dip recession. These numbers have to be provisional; following past experience, they may be revised upwards. But he won't hit his self-proclaimed aim that in 2015–16 debt will fall as a share of GDP. Blaming Europe for failure came naturally, but was triply unconvincing. First of all, as a matter of fact, UK exports to the EU had been growing, at least until early 2012. Secondly, the deepening Eurozone crisis was in large measure a result of the same austerity policies Osborne and Cameron insisted were the remedy for the UK. And thirdly, if the Eurozone crisis was as bad for Britain as Osborne claimed, wasn't that the best reason to temper austerity and revive demand?

But thinking again is for pragmatists. Cameron's stiff-necked insistence on sticking with his cuts may show that despite the haplessness and chaos, his inner ideological core is steely. Shrinkage was and remains his government's guiding light and so far, just about, public opinion has bought the case for cuts, though polls on voting intentions have turned sharply against the Tories. Cameron cuts will permanently damage and diminish the state, and in that sense he may yet leave the field a winner.

But he has yet to deliver the planned cuts. The IFS reckoned that, at April 2012, four-fifths of reductions had still to be realized. Departments and public bodies had lopped the easiest to reach branches, cancelling investment, freezing pay. The body count must now rise. In 2011, 270,000 public sector staff were sacked, cutting the payroll by 7 per cent. By March 2012, according to Unison estimates, 625 public employees were losing their jobs every day, and decimation must go on indefinitely. Osborne's targets depend on chopping cash support for the disabled, further cuts in tax credits – which make low-paid work even less attractive – and paying less housing benefit, which forces population movements that make no economic or social sense.

Can Cameron stay the course? His second act script was presented in rarely scrutinized business plans for Whitehall departments.[43] But within weeks of their publication in June

2012, ambitions were being abandoned. Take the Treasury's aim of greater variation in public sector pay, meaning those who work for councils, DWP or the NHS in poorer parts of the country would see their salaries cut so the private sector employers can then cut their pay scales too. Tory MPs grew alarmed; local business people disputed the Treasury's understanding of labour markets; in the civil service reform white paper, regional pay variation was nowhere to be found. It hangs in the air uncertainly.

In a remarkable speech Osborne rounded on business for failing to speak out in favour of tax cuts.[44] The unwillingness of business to be as Thatcherite as the government would like may prove a growing problem. Business was notably reticent over stripping employees of rights, which may mean BIS will find it hard to implement the Cameron-backed plan to allow managers to fire at will. Duncan Smith may learn a lesson you could read long before the welfare state was created: in trying to help poor households there's a permanent trade-off between simplicity and fairness. The Work Programme will look even more like a perilous privatization if contractors demand to be paid despite failing to find clients jobs that aren't there.

Despite a pre-election pledge of a bigger army, 25,000 are to be cut from the services and 29,000 civilian staff as the Ministry of Defence budget is to shrink by 7.5 per cent by 2015. But that is not matched by any slimming in UK pretension. If the state must be urgently reduced, why go on spending twice as large a proportion of GDP on defence as Germany, a higher proportion than the Chinese (officially) spend, clinging to the top table, the UK's permanent seat on the UN security council seat and a role as rear gunner in any passing war? The armed forces are not presumably being maintained just to pick up the pieces when private Olympics security contractors fail to deliver.

The government, according to the defence business plan, will 'succeed in Afghanistan' (whatever that means); 'continue to fulfil its standing commitments' (tautology); promote defence exports (while cutting its own purchases); 'succeed in other operations it is required to undertake' (obeying prime ministerial whim). The MOD has now started buying elements of the renewed Trident system, for which the lowest total estimate is £20 billion, an unexplained, luxury survivor in these years of austerity.

From the Department for Communities and Local Government business plan springs an extraordinary proposal to identify 120,000 troubled families and sort them out. Evidence for the existence of a permanent core of disadvantaged households is shaky; ministers talk about families in trouble, families causing trouble and troubled families, though the categories and numbers are all different. Whitehall wants councils to seek them out and earn £4,000 if they get mothers and fathers into jobs and sons and daughters into school, stop them offending, or causing neighbours trouble – all this while their benefits are being cut and in-work rewards falling for those in work.

The government hopes to bask in an Olympic glow, but culture and sports policy will be paralysed until Jeremy Hunt leaves his ministerial role. His department's business plans still look ominous as their stated intention is to deregulate broadcasting and communications and keep up pressure on the BBC to 'ensure it is more accountable'. The BBC appointed a new director-general, George Entwistle, amid Tory attacks, the Mayor of London, Boris Johnson, having publicly demanded the appointee be a Tory. A Tory of a different stamp, the chair of the BBC Trust, Lord Chris Patten held firm and appointed on merit.

In education, the government plans to bring more private money into schools through sponsorship, compel more primaries to become academies and fragment the system further as Free and Studio Schools expand and, in some areas, a revamped version of the old city technology colleges is established. In justice they are turning offender management upside down, bringing more private contractors into prisons, probation and community sentences; they do not explain why private companies will stop the growth in prison numbers that, on the face of things, would bring the private jailers extra income.

The Department of Environment and Climate Change business plan says, though not in these terms, it will try to cope with the negative consequences of privatization under a previous Tory government: lack of a national water grid, excessive leakage and inadequate sewerage in London. They also need to reform the energy market: a dearth of bidders to build new nuclear power and nimby Tory MPs blocking wind farms combine to show the limits of a privatized market and what happens when there is no strategic direction from ministers.

Nothing is joined up. Transport Department plans for charging heavy goods vehicles to use the roads would make sense if they were married to a programme of shifting freight to rail and radically cutting the number of journeys being made by retail companies. The point of the previous privatizations of rail and buses was to break them up and, besides, the business plan's aim of 'making public transport more attractive' is unlikely to be implemented when fares are rising faster than inflation.

In health the Tories face daunting political risks. Voters may not absorb administrative detail but one thing they know: Cameron promised during the 2010 election not to cut or privatize the NHS. He may achieve a stand-still budget but health never stands still: pressure grows. As the system is deliberately fragmented, it will fail to cope with new crises, such as controlling the explosion in diabetes.[45] At the 2010 Tory Party conference, Francis Maude said the government was relaxed about creating a postcode lottery for healthcare and other services, and that is precisely what will result: as the state is rolled back, there can be no national standards. The public always strongly resents any suggestion they can get a drug or treatment in one place, but not another. New evidence emerges of the centrality of mental health, and how switching resources to psychological services could save large sums from physical healthcare budgets. But that would mean a national initiative, with the capacity to steer and reallocate. In opposition Cameron derided Labour's targets but has sought to reimpose the same eighteen-week maximum wait for surgery – demonstrating how often he finds centralism essential when faced with the consequences of the anarchy that characterizes his competition policy.

When you've provoked thousands of police constables to give up off-duty time to march through Whitehall in vocal opposition to your plans for their pay and pensions as they did in May 2012, you might take care not to rile them further. They are, after all, the people you are going to depend on to police the other demos, to put down riots and reassure the public on crime. But no, the Cameron recipe for policing is turmoil. He is simultaneously cutting police numbers, overhauling recruitment and promotion, appointing a detested hatchet man as Chief Inspector of Constabulary, reorganizing the national detective agencies and, to crown it all, creating elected commissioners, who will have a built-in incentive to slug it out with chief constables, interfere with police operations – and harry the government for more crime-fighting resources.

If you wanted a three-word badge for Cameron's first half, it would be Any Qualified Provider. The Open Public Services white paper published in July 2011 expresses their radicalism. It was to have been published in February that year but a scandal at Winterbourne View, a long-term private residential hospital, provoked alarm at private profiteering. Undeterred, Letwin and

Maude, Gauleiters for the policy, went ahead and published the master plan a few months later. The default position for all public services is private provision, and not even the military or policing is exempt. Most services will be obliged to drum up at least three rivals, preferably commercial, to bid for every service. Cameron told the Tory spring conference in 2011 he wanted to create a new presumption against the dead hand of the state.[46] Woe betide any civil servant obstructing it: 'If I have to pull those people into my office and get them off the backs of business, then believe me I'll do it.'

It's working. 'The UK's austerity programme is entering a fruitful phrase for outsourcing,' said an analyst in June 2012, noting £4 billion worth of government work out to tender in the first six months of the year alone.[47] The Tories intend irreversible change, believing that once they excavate the foundations, this edifice can't be rebuilt. Whether they get enough time to complete the demolition depends in part on manipulating the constitution, for example by shrinking the House of Commons so they gain MPs and the other parties lose. They benefit from the failure to agree fair funding of political parties as they block a reform to take giant donations out of the system. They benefit from switching to individual from household registration of voters, while Labour loses many poorer voters off the lists. They will ensure no House of Lords reform removes their age-old natural majority among the peers.

But success also depends on their administrative and political ability. Both have proved surprisingly weak so far. Their sheer determination to push through NHS commercialization in the face of vocal opposition shows that beneath the surface bungling there is a core of steel, but recklessness over how things work could stop them in their tracks.

There are other countervailing tendencies. Philosophically,

Conservatism is all over the place. Shrink-the-state zeal conflicts with a Tory desire to keep Britain great with over-the-odds defence spending. Love of the little platoons of localism vies with the constant urge to command. Market freedom is at odds with social order and, for example, Cameron's National Citizens Service for the young. Ministers rubbish professionalism, abuse the civil service, slander GPs and teachers. As they appoint a lawyer keen on privatization to be HM Chief Inspector of Constabulary, how willingly will officers put their lives on the line in future? Even a shrunken state needs disinterested, enthusiastic public servants.

In the second half, governing will get harder. Liberal Democrats facing electoral annihilation will have to consider an early exit from the coalition. For a shard of electoral credibility they will start demanding a new economic plan, but Cameron will not relish an early election with no sign of the green shoots of recovery.

Another question will press. Osborne dared not repeat his line about all being in this together when he cut tax for the rich in his 2012 budget. As benefit cuts bite and real incomes fall, the unjust distribution of pain gets plainer for all to see. For all his speeches on social justice and social mobility, the thrust of Cameron policy is to make the country more unequal at an accelerating pace. By 2015, the IFS estimates, at least 500,000 more children will fall below the official poverty threshold: this compares badly with Labour, who took a million out of poverty. Duncan Smith's think-tank is working overtime on trying to show poverty is only a socialist construct, and that official measures based on income are worthless. They won't succeed as the accumulating data show the young, women and the poorest households have taken a disproportionate share of the cuts. Geographically, socially, financially, educationally and electorally, Cameron has favoured his own people. For example, the National Commissioning Board for health is no longer obliged to share out money according to the indices of deprivation; resources are being 'equalized', which means redirecting funds from poorer areas in the North of England to richer southern districts.

In the end electors will judge on the economy. Euro-cataclysm may precipitate a wider collapse and Osborne will try hard to blame the EU for the added economic damage caused by his austerity. Economists warn of a decade or even two of depression, stagnation and socially unsustainable unemployment. Cameron could still change course, responding to unfolding events with imagination and humility. But that would mean abandoning the project that his Tory generation picked up from Thatcher, their vendetta against government and their unshakeable trust in markets, despite all the evidence of failure and perverse consequences. Such a volte-face is unlikely, so Cameron's second half offers more of the same dogma and disarray.

Notes

1. *Economist*, 20 January 2011.
2. http://www.guardian.co.uk/uk/2012/mar/10/rising-crime-police-cuts-conservative-labour
3. House of Commons Public Administration Select Committee, 11th report of Session 2010–12.
4. http://www.bbc.co.uk/news/uk-politics-12163624
5. *Guardian*, 11 March 2005.
6. http://www.guardian.co.uk/society/joepublic/2011/sep/27/new-public-policies-test
7. http://www.independent.co.uk/life-style/health-and-families/health-news/letwin-nhs-will-not-exist-under-tories-6168295.html
8. http://www.brandrepublic.com/news/1051960/
9. http://www.guardian.co.uk/politics/2011/feb/01/big-society-lord-wei-volunteering
10. http://www.guardian.co.uk/politics/2012/mar/25/peter-cruddas-resigns-cash-access
11. House of Lords Science and Technology Select Committee, 2nd report of Session 2010–12.
12. http://www.guardian.co.uk/education/2012/apr/23/free-schools-deprived-pupils-average
13. David Laws and Paul Marshall (eds), *The Orange Book*, Profile Books 2004.
14. Timothy Heppell and David Seawright, *Cameron and the Conservatives*, Macmillan 2012, p. 15.
15. *Progress magazine*, May 2012 special supplement.
16. http://www.guardian.co.uk/politics/2010/may/25/queen-s-speech-debate-david-cameron-attacks-labour

17. Polly Toynbee and David Walker, *The Verdict: Did Labour Change Britain?*, Granta 2010.
18. IFS, *Green Budget*, 2011, p. 79.
19. *Financial Times*, 2 October 2009.
20. *Financial Times*, 2–3 June 2012.
21. *Daily Telegraph*, 5 April 2012.
22. *Financial Times*, 24 May 2012, p. 6.
23. *Times*, 24 May 2012, p. 19.
24. See *Financial Times*, 1 June 2012 p. 22.
25. *Financial Times*, 12 May 2012.
26. http://www.cable.co.uk/news/former-bt-cto-slams-unambitious-broadband-plans-801322915/
27. http://www.nao.org.uk/publications/1213/regional_growth_fund.aspx
28. *Financial Times*, 24 May 2012.
29. http://www.guardian.co.uk/society/2012/jun/21/nhs-boss-incredulous-andrew-lansley
30. http://www.ft.com/cms/s/0/f9d96824-7a71-11df-9cd7-00144feabdc0.html#axzz16P30Yfay
31. http://www.guardian.co.uk/politics/2011/may/14/david-cameron-adviser-health-reform
32. http://www.guardian.co.uk/politics/2012/mar/04/nhs-watchdog-ccp-lord-carter
33. www.ilcuk.org.uk/files/pdf_pdf_124.pdf
34. http://www.instituteforgovernment.org.uk/sites/default/files/publications/One%20Year%20On_0.pdf
35. www.guardian.co.uk/politics/2012/may/29/michael-gove-open-state-schools-profit?newsfeed=true
36. *Financial Times*, 9 May 2012, p. 4.
37. http://www.publications.parliament.uk/pa/cm201012/cmselect/cmpubacc/1957/195703.htm
38. http://www.spectator.co.uk/coffeehouse/7855598/the-unions-versus-the-department-for-education-continued.thtml
39. *Guardian*, 23 June 2012, p. 17.
40. http://www.timeshighereducation.co.uk/story.asp?storycode=415322
41. http://uk.reuters.com/article/2012/06/21/uk-britain-cameron-g-idUKBRE85K0XJ20120621
42. *BBC News*, 1 May 2012.
43. http://www.cabinetoffice.gov.uk/news/business-plans-show-government-delivering-radical-reform-across-public-services
44. http://www.ft.com/cms/s/0/7df036b2-b4bb-11e1-bb2e-00144feabdc0.html#axzz1ydCc2lp8
45. http://www.publications.parliament.uk/pa/cm201213/cmselect/cmpubacc/uc289-i/uc28901.htm
46. http://www.telegraph.co.uk/news/politics/8364843/David-Cameron-go-getters-will-save-economy.html
47. *Financial Times*, 18 June 2012, p. 4.

Index

INDEX